WOMEN OF COLOR DEVOTIONAL BOOK

© 2002 by Nia Publishing

All Scripture quotes, unless otherwise indicated, are from the Authorized King James Version of the Bible.

Scripture quotes marked NIV are taken from the HOLY BIBLE, NEW INTERNATIONAL VERSION®. Copyright© 1973, 1978, 1984 by the International Bible Society.

NIA PUBLISHING is an African-American owned company based in Atlanta, GA. Started in 1993 by Mel Banks, Jr., former market-ing director for Urban Ministries, Inc., its first product was *The Children of Color Bible.* Nia has recently produced the *Wisdom and Grace Bible for Young Women of Color* and the *Men of Color Study Bible.* The ownership, employees, and products of Nia Publishing are dedicated and committed to the cultural and spiritual growth of people of color, as individuals in the community and in the church. Nia can be visited on the internet at *www.niapublishing.com.*

Produced by the Livingstone Corporation. Project staff include: Mary Horner Collins, Joan Guest, Greg Longbons, Jan Ord, Anthony Platipodis, and Linda Taylor.

Some material has been taken from the *Women of Color Devotional Bible,* copyright © 2002 by Nia Publishing.

ISBN 0-529-11577-8

Published in cooperation with:

World Bible Publishers, Inc.
Iowa Falls, IA 50126
U.S.A.

Manufactured in the United States of America

1 2 3 4 5 6 7 8 **DPI** 08 07 06 05 04 03 02

Contents

The Love of God

JAN HALL-LUNN

But God commendeth his love toward us,

in that, while we were yet sinners,

Christ died for us.

Romans 5:8

My Creator, my Savior, my Lord

"ESTHER," DEBRA SAID AFTER STOPPING over to visit, "I believe that daughter of yours is going to preach the Word of God someday. I declare, when she prays just about every hair on the back of my neck stands up. I get goose bumps."

Esther smiled before she spoke. "Praise the Lord, Debra, she is in that Bible studying every chance she gets. This is the direction God seems to be pulling her. Listen! She's in her room praying up something right now."

"God," Esther's daughter prayed, "it is you who makes provision for me. It is not my job or my status in life that opens doors for me. You have provided for me when there was no job. You have kept a roof over my head, food on my table, clothes on my back, and even my car to drive. So God, I have learned to love you as *Jehovah-Jireh,* the God who provides. When storm clouds are raging and trouble is on every side, you lead me to the Rock that is higher than I; that is how I came to know you as *Jehovah-Shalom,* my peace. Father God, you have been so faithful and have kept every promise that you have made to your people. You loved us enough to send your only Son to be the atonement for our sins. If we searched the whole world over, we would find none like you anywhere, for you are the only righteous One; that's how I grew to love you as *Jehovah-Tsidkenu,* my righteousness.

The ladies listened intently as Esther's daughter finished her prayer. "Hallelujah, Esther, the Lord is really using that girl. Now that prayer ought to have the attention of heaven."

How many times have we given our love to people who did not want it, did not appreciate it, or just abused it? Consider a loving God, our heavenly Father, who has promised to always love us, never to leave us, and never to forsake us, even when we don't deserve it.

As the prayer above said, he will lovingly provide for our needs. He loves us so much that he sent his only Son to walk among us so that he could know our pain and could identify with our sinful nature. He took on himself all of our suffering and sin, yet he himself was without sin. He took our sin to the cross, dying so we might live. This is the epitome of love, in that while we were yet sinners, Christ died for us.

Prayer

Dear God, thank you for your great love. As the psalmist said: "I will bless the Lord at all times. His praise shall continually be in my mouth." Father, I adore you and love you. Help me pass your love on to others. In the wonderful name of Jesus, I pray. Amen.

Something to Ponder

DESCRIBE THE KIND OF LOVE YOU WANT TO GIVE TO PEOPLE IN YOUR LIFE.

Faith

TREVY A. MCDONALD

But without faith it is impossible to please
him: for he that cometh to God must believe
that he is, and that he is a rewarder of them
that diligently seek him.

Hebrews 11:6

What is this thing called faith?

"IMANI! I HAVEN'T SEEN YOU IN AGES," Justine exclaimed from the canned food aisle in the grocery store. She embraced Imani with a bear hug.

"Mommy, who is that?" Justine's six-year-old daughter inquired.

"I'm one of your Mommy's friends from high school," Imani shared. "Can you believe it's been 15 years?"

Justine nodded. "I know! Well, what are you up to, girl? Where have you been?"

"Actually I just moved back home. After college I worked my way up the ladder at a computer firm, but they were recently hit hard and I was let go. So I moved back home. I thought there might be more opportunity here than in a smaller city."

"Not a bad idea," Justine paused and reached for a can of peaches. "Say Imani, I'm surprised I haven't seen you on the big screen yet. You were dynamic in our school plays and you were always creating plays when we were growing up."

"True, but I've been out of the loop too long. And where would I start?"

"Chicago has become a hotbed for film production. You should go to some auditions. You never know what might happen. By the way, is the number at your parents' house still the same?"

"Yes."

"I'll be checking up on you. Use this time to realize your dream."

"But how?"

"Just pray about it, ask God to order your steps, and step out on faith. You'll be in the right place at the right time." Justine looked down at her watch. "Look, I better run," Justine embraced Imani. "I promise I'll be in touch."

What is this thing called faith? In Hebrews 11:1 we are told, "faith is the substance of things hoped for, the evidence of things not seen." In essence, faith is our most basic need.

For Christians, having faith means believing what we can't see because we know the Lord will direct our paths and supply our needs. We have all, at some point in our lives, desired something. Perhaps your desire was so strong that you left the former without the new in sight. The naysayers said you had lost your mind, but you knew it was time because you had faith in God to direct you. You were certain of what was not yet in sight and positive that it was far better than what was behind you. Some said you were taking a risk, but you left your comfort zone and stepped out on faith.

Prayer

Dear heavenly Father, whose omniscience directs me, I thank you for your most perfect and precious gift, your Son, whom you sent to this world for my salvation. Sometimes I get so caught up in my daily comfort zone that I lose sight of my hopes and dreams. They seem distant and unattainable. Lord, I find comfort in knowing your promises are certain. Enable me each day to grow in the knowledge that I can trust in you and anticipate the fulfillment of your promises. In Jesus' name, I pray. Amen.

Something to Ponder

THE NEXT TIME YOU HAVE TO EXERCISE FAITH IN GOD IN YOUR LIFE, HOW WILL YOU DO IT?

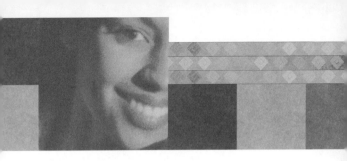

Forgiveness

KAREN L. WADDLES

If we confess our sins, he is faithful and just to
forgive us our sins, and to cleanse us from all
unrighteousness.

> *1 John 1:9*

God's extended mercy

IT WAS 1:00 IN THE MORNING AND THE AIR was heavy with smells of cheap perfume, cigar and cigarette smoke, and liquor. There was a chill in the breeze that caused her to pull at the hem of her very short skirt. She hadn't done well tonight—but the night was young.

As she rounded the corner, she almost walked into him. "Excuse me, Sir…are you looking for a party girl?" she asked. He paused and spoke slowly, "I would like to have some of your time this evening. Why don't we walk." Something about his voice made her agree. As they walked for the next hour she felt his eyes piercing almost to her soul and hoped he wasn't put off by her appearance and her lifestyle.

He wasn't. She told him about a life that had driven her to the streets. He told her about a man named Jesus who died to pay for all her sins. "You're forgiven," he said.

"But you don't know what I've—"

"Forgiven," he repeated. "He paid for the shame, the guilt, the stain of sin—you are forgiven." In those few words she found the peace she had sought for so long. As she accepted this Savior, she knew that her life would never be the same.

Real forgiveness is a difficult concept for us to grasp with our finite minds. We rank sins from little "white lies" to really big sins. We are prone to hold grudges and keep a tally card for infractions made against us. Yet Christ promises that when we confess our sins to him, he remembers them no more (Jeremiah 31:34).

For the unbeliever there is no greater message. We can bring to Christ our tattered, broken, abused hearts and lives, and place ourselves at his feet. We can acknowledge our sin and need for a Savior, and he promises to forgive, pardon and cleanse. He died on Calvary's cross to pay for every sin—there is no condemnation to those who are in Christ Jesus (Romans 8:1)!

For the believer the message is just as powerful. How often are we strapped under a tremendous weight of guilt and shame because of unconfessed sin in our lives? Satan loves to remind us that if we were really saved, we wouldn't do those things. And always, Christ is standing at the opposite end of the spectrum reminding us that it was for our sins he died on Calvary. He invites us to accept his offer of forgiveness. Stand beneath Calvary's flow and be washed and cleansed of all sin.

Prayer

Lord Jesus, I fall before you and offer you my broken life. I believe that you died for my sins. I accept your forgiveness, your full pardon, and ask that you wash me with your Word. Help me to know the fullness of my relationship with you. Amen.

Something to Ponder

WHO DO YOU NEED TO FORGIVE, AND WHAT WILL YOU SAY TO LET THAT PERSON KNOW HE/SHE IS FORGIVEN?

Mercy and Grace

ROBIN M. DIAL

And he said, I will make all my goodness pass before thee, and I will proclaim the name of the Lord before thee; and will be gracious to whom I will be gracious, and will shew mercy on whom I will shew mercy.

Exodus 33:19

God's grace and mercy towards me

SYLVIA AND MESHELL, BOTH ATTRACTIVE women in their mid-thirties, were on their regular monthly Saturday luncheon.

"I'm so blessed to have a friend like you," Meshell told Sylvia.

"Remember that God has placed us in each other's lives for a specific reason," Sylvia replied.

Meshell began to reminisce about the many times that Sylvia and her husband had taken in Meshell and the children after Meshell's husband had gone on one of his drunken rages. She remembered the time her oldest daughter had pleaded with her to remove them from their horrible situation.

Sylvia smiled sweetly at her friend. "Girl, we did a lot of fasting and praying for you to get out of that situation."

Meshell laughed before she spoke, "And you never stopped praying for me." After a thoughtful pause, Meshell confided again, "It would've been so easy for me to be jealous of how God had chosen to bless you in your life."

"Oh, but for God's grace and mercy toward me, your story could have easily been my story," Sylvia quickly responded.

Both Sylvia and Meshell thanked God for each of their experiences. Meshell finally said, "Sylvia, our circumstances have brought us both closer to Christ and to each other."

God will do just what he said he would do. You are where you are for a specific reason. God wants you to live for him and he wants all the glory and honor. Stop right now and read Exodus 33:19. God has promised to always give us just the amount of grace and mercy that we need. Your spiritual growth is most important to him. The trials and tribulations that you encounter are simply to make you stronger. Psalm 103:13 says, "Like as a father pitieth his children, so the Lord pitieth them that fear him."

Prayer

Dear heavenly Father, I come to you today thanking you for the many experiences that I go through. Each experience makes me stronger and brings me closer to you. I ask you to continue to pour out your grace and mercy on me and help me to grow spiritually. Thank you, Lord. Amen.

Something to Ponder

HOW CAN YOU BE MORE MERCIFUL TO OTHERS IN YOUR LIFE?

Revenge

SONNIE BEVERLY

For I reckon that the sufferings of this present
time are not worthy to be compared with the
glory which shall be revealed in us.

Romans 8:18

The suffering can't compare

NATALIE AND SHEILA WERE BEST FRIENDS. Natalie was nonconfrontational, plain looking, and had a boyfriend named Eddie. Sheila thought of herself as more beautiful than Natalie. She was a flirt, yet Sheila had no boyfriend.

The best friends were going shopping for swimsuits to wear to a neighborhood pool party. When Natalie arrived at Sheila's house, the door was open. Like many times before, Natalie walked right in. This time, though, Natalie overheard a conversation that Sheila was having with her sister. Sheila said that no matter what swimsuit Natalie bought, Sheila would look better. Sheila also said that Eddie thought she was finer than Natalie. She was sure she could take him from Natalie once he saw her in a swimsuit.

Natalie was hurt to the bone. How could her best friend say that about her and make such comments about her boyfriend? Feelings of hurt and betrayal overtook Natalie. She had a mind to get back at her by marching right in that kitchen and telling Sheila that she wasn't all that.

Retaliation is powerful, yet there is nothing more powerful than forgiveness. Several things can be done to resist the

temptation to retaliate, and be able to forgive instead. Because our natural instincts and reflexes usually lead us to strike back, we must immediately find the pause button and press it. We must take time to get our thoughts, words, and actions under control. As we pause, we must pray for the Holy Spirit to direct us.

The Bible says that our suffering can't compare to the glory that will be revealed in us. There will be times when we may suffer by the words or actions of others. However, during these times God promises that we can tap into the power of the Holy Spirit to gain strength to turn away from the temptation to sin. If we weigh our options, we will see that it is more beneficial to wait for the glory that will be revealed in us as daughters of God. When we do that, we can resist the temptation to retaliate.

As born-again believers, we are daughters of God, adopted into God's family. We can call him "Abba Father" (Romans 8:15). We have all the privileges and responsibilities of legitimate children, including the leadership of the Spirit. Even when we are wronged and it does not feel that we belong to God, the Holy Spirit is our witness. His inward presence reminds us of who we are and encourages us with God's love.

Prayer

Abba Father, I am very upset about what was done to me. Please help me find the pause button. No matter what someone else does to me, I don't want that to interfere with our relationship. My goal in this relationship is to make you smile. I don't feel like smiling right now because I am angry. I'm hurt. I feel betrayed and I want to lash back. Let me feel your presence in and around me so that it will overtake these negative feelings. Thank you, Daddy, for hearing my prayer and responding. In the name of my big brother, Jesus. Amen.

Something to Ponder

INSTEAD OF GIVING PEOPLE WHAT THEY DESERVE WHEN THEY DO YOU WRONG, HOW CAN YOU HANDLE THE SITUATION IN A GODLY MANNER?

Prayer

ALISE D. BARRYMORE

Thou knowest my downsitting and mine
uprising, thou understandest my thought afar
off. Thou compassest my path and my lying
down, and art acquainted with all my ways.
For there is not a word in my tongue, but, lo,
O Lord, thou knowest it altogether.

Psalm 139:2-4

Tired of talking

WHEN MARCIA CALLED HER GIRLFRIEND Nicole, she got a busy signal for the third time. Her frustration was rising by the moment. How could the line be busy? Nicole had three-way calling *and* call waiting. How could a person with so many access numbers—a pager, a cell phone, and voicemail at home and work—be so hard to find? Just a few more minutes and Marcia was going to give up. It didn't seem worth it. But she decided she would try one more time. Frustrated but desperate, Marcia punched her phone number and the emergency code 911 into the mobile messaging system. *Come on, answer,* she thought to herself. *I need you. I need to talk. Now.* But there was no return call that day. Just silence. *Where is a friend when you need one?* thought Marcia.

We often seek out answers to life's most pressing concerns by turning to a friend, loved one, or neighbor. We depend on others to ascribe meaning to our lives. When we reach the figurative end of our rope and have exhausted all of our inner resources, we search the landscape for a kind word, a gentle embrace, and some genuine understanding. This is not bad; it is often beneficial to consult others and to gain various perspectives.

However, sometimes people fail us. They may be too busy. They may tire of our story and have little time for our pain. At times they shut down or shut us out. Secretly we wonder if God is tired of listening to us, too. Does the God of heaven and earth attend to our seemingly miniscule situation? Does prayer even work? We imagine that God has a caller ID service and all of our calls are being ignored.

When you feel as though God is not listening, or you are simply tired of rehearsing your situation, it is okay to stop talking. Trust that God knows your heart. Believe that the God who sees your thoughts before you speak them is willing and able to interpret the muddle in your head. Pray in a new and different way today, and wait to hear God's response.

Prayer

Lord God, when I get tired of talking to you, please continue to talk with me. When I get weary of worship, please hear the unspoken cries of my heart. It is my desire to know you and to be known by you. Help me to hear from you. In Jesus' name. Amen.

Something to Ponder

IF YOU WROTE OUT A PRAYER TO GOD TODAY, WHAT WOULD IT SAY?

Miracles

MARJORIE L. KIMBROUGH

For the Father loveth the Son, and sheweth
him all things that himself doeth: and he will
shew him greater works than these, that ye
may marvel.

John 5:20

The miracle of sight

YEARS AGO IT WAS DETERMINED THAT MY seven-year-old son needed glasses. I took him to an ophthalmologist, and he was fitted for glasses. The morning after he got his glasses, he walked outside and announced in total surprise, "Mom, I can see across the street!" He did not know that most people could see across the street without glasses. Wearing glasses has been second nature to him for twenty-seven years now, but his eyes have been steadily deteriorating. He decided to have laser vision correction.

During this procedure pulses of light emitted from the laser surgically reshape the surface of the cornea using the same principles that eyeglasses and contact lenses use. My son's surgery was quite successful. He was able to see without his glasses immediately following the procedure, and the morning following the surgery he drove himself to the doctor for a checkup. The doctor was amazed by the amount of healing that had already taken place. Knowing that he would probably need a weaker prescription for glasses, my son asked the doctors for the new prescription. They informed him that he no longer needed glasses at all. The medical miracle was greater than he had dared to imagine!

Jesus promised that God would show us works so great that we would be astonished. He is a God of miracles. It is simply amazing to consider how God has designed our eyes and vision. It is overwhelming as well that human beings have developed the intelligence to mimic in a tiny way what God has done throughout creation. For God this process is natural; for us it is a miracle!

Prayer

Lord, thank you for the intelligence that allows men and women to scratch the surface of your miraculous design of the human body. But thank you more for the miracles you perform around us every day. Amen.

Something to Ponder

WHAT MIRACLE HAS GOD DONE IN YOUR LIFE?

Soul Mates

TARA GRIGGS-MAGEE

But from the beginning of the creation God
made them male and female. For this cause
shall a man leave his father and mother, and
cleave to his wife; and they twain shall be
one flesh: so then they are no more twain,
but one flesh.

> *Mark 10:6-8*

Waiting for God

I REMEMBER IT AS IF IT WERE YESTERDAY. I closed my eyes and prayed, "Lord, you really don't have to send him now, but please tell me, when will the man that you have for me come?"

Dare I rush God on such an important task? But, like so many sisters I knew at that time who saw age 30 coming right around the corner, I wondered what he was waiting for. Didn't God know about the biological clock that I felt was ticking away? "Knowing this, that the trying of your faith worketh patience. But let patience have her perfect work, that ye may be perfect and entire, wanting nothing" (James 1:3,4). Then I heard the Spirit of the Lord whisper softly in my ear that while I waited, he was not only preparing *me* for my soul mate, but also was preparing my mate for *me.* I learned at that very moment that if we learn to trust God and his perfect timing, then he will surely give us the desires of our hearts.

Now I can't attest to being a veteran of marriage. Lord knows that there are many who have tenure on me in this department; but I can truly say that I have a quality marriage with my soul mate, Willard, of close to nine years. Being a twenty-first century career couple and raising Trey, our beautiful four-year-old son, can get hectic, but we have a rhythm that is special. I know without a shadow of a doubt that I married the man that God prepared for me. We have both learned what mature love feels like after all of these years because our love continues to grow deeper every day. I can truly say that Willard and I are best friends, and I feel blessed to share my life with such a focused, strong, responsible, and loving man. If you could only see "my boys" together, you would know that I could not have a better husband and father for our son. I'm glad I waited for God's timing!

The secret to a great marriage is to trust and honor your spouse. It is important that you bring 100 percent of you into the marriage in order to make it work. Even 99 percent just won't do. Of course, your first love and commitment needs to be to our heavenly Father. Nothing should ever break that bond, not even marriage. God has to be at the head of your marriage. Without him, prepare for an extremely severe and bumpy ride.

Prayer

Lord God Almighty, I pray for wisdom as you teach me the importance of patience and waiting. Help me keep my mind stayed on thee during this time in my life as I wait for that which you have prepared for me. Lord, I will put nothing else before you. I want to grow deeper in your Word and learn to walk in your ways. I may not know what you have prepared for my future, but I will trust you no matter what. In the name of Jesus, I pray. Amen.

Something to Ponder

WHAT THINGS DO SOUL MATES HAVE TO DO TO
STAY STRONGLY CONNECTED TO ONE ANOTHER?

Marriage

MICHELE CLARK JENKINS

My brethren, count it all joy when ye fall into
divers temptations; Knowing this, that the trying
of your faith worketh patience. But let patience
have her perfect work, that ye may be perfect
and entire, wanting nothing. If any of you lack
wisdom, let him ask of God, that giveth to all
men liberally, and upbraideth not; and it shall be
given him. But let him ask in faith, nothing
wavering. For he that wavereth is like a wave of
the sea driven with the wind and tossed.

James 1:2-6

I wish, I wish, I wish

A WOMAN AND HER HUSBAND WERE approaching their tenth wedding anniversary. It had been a hard ten years. Soft, loving words had long been absent from their conversations with each other. Their intimate times were few and far between and were mechanical. Neither of them really knew if the other was being faithful and, truth be told, neither really cared. They avoided talking about important things, and most of their conversations became arguments that led to degrading remarks, name-calling, and accusations.

They both professed to love the Lord, but neither knew the depth of faith the other had because they never shared their faith on an intimate level. They had tried going to a marriage counselor, but it didn't work and just gave each of them more ammunition. She'd gotten to the point where she couldn't watch another couple walk down the street holding hands or watch a romantic movie without crying. A happy marriage was no longer a hope or prayer. Now she would settle for a civil relationship with her material needs being met. But when she was all alone with God, she wondered, *Is this all that you have for me?*

All of us want to be "happy." But we need to differentiate fleeting moments of feeling happy from true lasting happiness. Happy feelings can be deceptive and can change to some other feelings without a moment's notice. The difference between maturity and immaturity is primarily acting on what we know instead of acting on what we feel. We are easily deceived by our feelings. When we feel unhappy or discontent, we often try to fix or change things.

"I'm unhappy in my marriage, so I'll go find happiness with another man."

"I'm unhappy in my marriage, so I'll find happiness by divorcing my husband."

"I'm unhappy in my marriage, so I'm going to change my husband into the man I want him to be and then I'll be happy."

"I'm unhappy in my marriage, so I'll go find happiness in _____.

What's your answer? If it is anything but Jesus, the answer will fail and you'll soon find yourself answering the same question again in another set of circumstances.

True lasting happiness is joy that comes from the peace of the Lord. When we have that peace and joy, we are like mighty oaks whose roots go deep (Isaiah 61:3). We do not sway in the wind from one emotion to the next. We know that each of us is a work in progress and that, just like labor pains, whatever we are going through will birth us anew, stronger and happier than before.

Prayer

Lord, you came to bind my broken heart and free me from the oppression in my life. You came to rebuild and renew my marriage and restore the places in it that have been long devastated. So now, Lord, I ask to receive a double portion for my husband, our marriage, and for myself. Let everlasting joy be ours. In your precious name, I pray. Amen.

Something to Ponder

WHAT DO YOU THINK AN IDEAL CHRISTIAN MARRIAGE LOOKS LIKE?

Celibacy

LINDA PEAVY

Flee fornication. Every sin that a man doeth is
without the body; but he that committeth fornication sinneth against his own body. What? know
ye not that your body is the temple of the Holy
Ghost which is in you, which ye have of God,
and ye are not your own? For ye are bought with
a price; therefore glorify God in your body, and
in your spirit, which are God's.

1 Corinthians 6:18-20

Talk to the hand!

DRIVING HOME FROM THEIR SINGLES' Ministry class, Dorothy asked her friend Audrey what she thought about the topic of the meeting that evening.

"Audrey, can you believe we were discussing celibacy? Please, girl, talk to the hand! There is no way in this day and age that I could possibly be celibate. And, by the way, I didn't believe Laurie when she said she was celibate. Come on now, do you *really* believe a woman can be celibate nowadays? With all of the temptation present and pressures placed upon women, I say no way."

Audrey softly replied, "Well, Dorothy, to be honest with you, it is possible. I know, because I'm celibate."

"Audrey, no!" shouted Dorothy.

"What do you mean, 'No'?" asked Audrey. "I'm not *dying;* I'm celibate."

"How is that possible, Audrey? You don't look celibate!"

First Corinthians 7:34 states that "the unmarried woman careth for the things of the Lord, that she may be holy both

in body and in spirit."Being committed to celibacy is a way of celebrating the body and the spirit. It is an example of holiness. We are all called by God to abstain from sexual impurity (1 Corinthians 6:18). But true celibacy, abstinence from sexual intercourse in order to serve God, is not a decision to be taken lightly. It requires much prayer and fasting. It is a promise you make to God and to yourself to honor the laws God has laid before you.

In your relationships with significant others, you need to ask yourself if you are honoring God. Are your actions pleasing in God's sight? Whether or not you become celibate is a decision only you can make. But in the meantime, a reexamination of your relationships is worthy of attention. Asking yourself why you are in a relationship or why you are engaging in certain activities is a good start. What pleasures are you deriving from your actions? Are these pleasures short-term or long-term, and do they fulfill the body or the spirit, or both?

Prayer

Oh heavenly Lord, my Savior and my source of strength, I choose you to guide me in my actions. Search me, Lord. Help me examine the desires and needs of my heart. Please don't allow me to fill the yearnings of my heart with frivolous and lustful musings that only last for a moment. But you, Lord, are able to fill every corner of my heart with an everlasting joy that surpasses all understanding. Help me to explore ways in which I can better please you. In the name of the Holy One, Christ Jesus. Amen.

Something to Ponder

HOW DO YOU KNOW WHEN GOD IS SPEAKING TO YOU?

True Beauty

CATHY ANN JOHNSON

Favour is deceitful, and beauty is vain:

but a woman that feareth the Lord,

she shall be praised.

Proverbs 31:30

Time out for beauty

TODAY WE ARE BOMBARDED WITH advertising promotions and promises of improving our physical appearance. There are products that change the texture of our hair, lighten our skin, remove cellulite, enhance our breasts, whiten our teeth, smooth the wrinkles in our face, improve the appearance of our hands, and the list goes on. To sum it all up, manufacturers have created a beauty-pageant image that my sistahs, myself included, have developed a strong desire to fulfill.

We sistahs who embrace this so-called notion of beauty spend a great deal of time and money shopping, researching, reading, and experimenting with new methods and products. How many times have you spent your Saturday in the mall shopping for the right dress, the right shoes, the right fragrance, stockings, hair solvents, nails, or jewelry? Come on girlfriends, stay with me. I am all for a woman putting her best foot forward; however, there comes a time when we sistahs need to take time out for *real* beauty. We need to rebuild what is on the inside. We need to rekindle our heritage, fast, pray, meditate, and resolve challenges in our lives. We need to give thanks, praise, and worship to the Lord.

Let's take a look at Queen Esther. Esther was invited to join an official beauty pageant. Visualize what this was like: Esther, a young Jewish girl, was placed in a harem filled with the most beautiful women in the land. These women had the finest perfumes, jewelry, and clothes available. I am talking about a serious day spa. They had phenomenal wardrobe designers, servants, dietitians, and instructors grooming them to physical perfection. Can you imagine the spiritual nature of these women? Imagine the vanity, the superficial attitudes, self-indulgence, and the egotistical spirits floating through this harem of divas. You get the picture? Does this remind you of any circumstances you may have experienced in modern day times—on television, in church, in school, or on the job?

In the midst of all this, there is Esther, whose inner beauty, strength, and dignity dominated the extravaganza. Esther's outer beauty was obvious, but her inner beauty could not be ignored. She seized the fascination of the king's eunuch, Hegai, who took her under his wing. With all her beauty and the favor given to her by Hegai, Esther still remained levelheaded. She focused on the inner qualities that radiated beyond her physical attributes. Her teachable spirit and her virtue of obedience won the king's heart and she became queen.

Prayer

Lord, thank you for allowing me to take time out for true inner beauty. Help me to recognize the beauty you give us within and to build on the uniqueness you have blessed me with. Make me discontent with being superficial. Deepen the desire to develop and cultivate the godly virtues that will honor you. Amen.

Something to Ponder

GOD USED ESTHER TO SAVE THE JEWS. WHAT IS HE CALLING YOU TO DO "IN SUCH A TIME AS THIS" (ESTHER 4:14)?

Courage to Heal

CYNTHIA D. BALLENGER

Wait on the Lord: be of good courage,

and he shall strengthen thine heart: wait,

I say, on the Lord.

Psalm 27:14

Healing from loss

JESSICA HAD ONLY BEEN MARRIED FOR TWO years, but because she was 28-years old when she got married, she was in a hurry to have children. Well, it finally happened! To her surprise, when she found out she was pregnant, it was a bittersweet feeling. Oh, she was happy; but the realization set in of the awesome responsibility ahead for her and her husband. They came to terms with it and began looking forward to their baby.

In the fifth month of her pregnancy, however, a regularly scheduled doctor's appointment led to heartache and grief. She found out that the baby had died; she couldn't miscarry but would have to have a stillborn birth. No explanation, no reason why it happened—it just happened. She felt as if her life was over. She thought, *How will I find the courage to heal through this loss?*

Jessica felt that her whole world was turned upside down. Her husband couldn't console her. Her mother and father couldn't console her. None of her friends could console her. What she needed was the courage to heal. Where would she find it? Who could possibly heal her broken heart?

You see, we women often think we must meet each challenge head-on by ourselves. At a young age most of us learned to cook, clean, and sew. One thing that is not often taught is "crisis intervention." In most cases we were taught to be self-sufficient. Subconsciously it's in our thinking to just press on. We must learn to lean on the Courage-giver, who is Christ. Without him there is no way to have the courage to heal and move on with our lives after a deep loss.

The key to finding the courage to heal is having an intimate relationship with God. Cry out to God and he will hear you (Psalm 18:1-6). When nobody else can hear, he does. Another thing we must do is allow others in our lives. Don't push away people who love you. When you are in such a delicate state, it's imperative to know that others love you and are praying for you.

Waiting on the Lord requires courage. It requires us to take stock of where we are in him and in what direction we are headed. Like Jessica, many women face the sadness of losing a child. Oh, how we need Jesus to bring us through. Jesus provides the comfort, guidance, and strength we need to find the courage to heal!

Prayer

Dear Jesus, I cry out to you right now and ask that you save me from myself. Remove all of the bad and replace it with your good! You are my rock, my fortress, and my deliverer, the God in whom I trust. Thank you for making your presence known while I go through this troubling time in my life. Amen.

Something to Ponder

WHAT ARE FIVE WAYS YOU CAN HEAL?

Peace

RACHELLE HOLLIE GUILLORY

Thou wilt keep him in perfect peace, whose mind is stayed on thee: because he trusteth in thee.

Isaiah 26:3

Peace of mind

ONE MORNING TWO FRIENDS WERE talking. "What's wrong, Denise? You sound unhappy," asked Lois.

Denise responded, "My doctor said I have an ulcer because I've been worrying too much. My mind is overwhelmed with all of my problems. I can't find peace anywhere. I don't know what to do."

Lois offered, "Have you tried giving it to Jesus? Trust in him and he'll give you peace of mind. Take your burdens to the altar and leave them there."

A little irritated, Denise responded, "I've done that. And as soon as I turn around from the altar, my burdens run behind me yelling, 'You ain't leavin' us here. We came together and we're leaving together!'"

Lois laughed, "Girl, I know. But as soon as they start creeping behind your back, know that God always has your back! You must constantly give your burdens to Jesus. It's a constant process."

The secret to peace of mind is wholly trusting in God and keeping your mind constantly on him. Of course, this does not mean that you should never think about anything other than God—that is neither possible nor logical. But in your

every decision, action, and reaction, you should consider the way and will of Christ and his divine purpose for your life. Then put your absolute trust in him—therein you will find perfect peace!

When your troubles are beyond your understanding, you should earnestly and humbly pray to God for peace, doing so with thanksgiving. God will grant you peace that exceeds all understanding (Philippians 4:6,7). Walking in peace is a constant process and it requires faith. Study your Bible daily. You are transformed by the renewing of your mind (Romans 12:2). Allow God to totally occupy your mind— peace will be yours!

Prayer

Lord, in your unique, unequaled, and matchless name, I now humbly bow in your presence. I need peace of mind, Jesus. It seems as if there is a war going on in my mind. So I now petition and welcome you to occupy and dwell in my mind. Take complete residence therein that I might experience the perfect peace which your Word promises. Amen.

Something to Ponder

WHAT IS A PEACEFUL DAY TO YOU?

Friendship

JESSICA H. LOVE

Iron sharpeneth iron; so a man sharpeneth
the countenance of his friend.

Proverbs 27:17

A friend in deed...

THROUGH THE DAILY ACTIVITIES OF MY JOB as a lawyer, I witness individuals fighting to save their lives through the legal system after being charged with destroying someone else's life, financially or emotionally. Too many times their trouble starts and stops with those whom they have defined as a "friend." As friends, they may have had a spoken or unspoken vow that they will be there for one another, regardless of the situation. They walk with superficial confidence, believing the words of their friend(s) when they say, "I got your back." It isn't until trouble comes that they realize it's every man for himself. Disappointed and frustrated, the blinders come off and they begin to realize that they never had a real friend.

The first step to determining whether or not you have a friend is knowing what a friend is. To know what a friend is or should be, go to the Bible and see God's definition. God tells us a friend is one who: acts as your intercessor when you are surrounded by trouble (Job 16:21); is always there for you during the good times and the bad (Proverbs 17:17); will stick closer to you than a brother (18:24); will hurt you with the truth, telling you what you need to hear, not what you want to hear (27:6); will bring out the best in you

(27:17); is there to help you up when you are knocked down by the storms of life (Ecclesiastes 4:10). In 1 Samuel 20, we are told of a story that epitomizes the word "friend." Despite the risk involved and the disapproval of their friendship by some, David and Jonathan had a friendship like none other; they truly had each other's back!

Who are those you call "friend"? Whose definition are you using, the world's or the Word's? Although we know God is the only Friend who can meet our every need, he will place people in your life you can call "friend." When he does, treat them like the blessing that they are. Prayerfully you will become a true friend to others, too.

Prayer

Lord, thank you for letting me know what a friend really is. Give me the wisdom and discernment to know friend from foe. If I have defined someone as a friend that doesn't meet your definition, reveal it to me. If I have befriended someone who will eventually bring trouble my way, I ask that you intercede on my behalf and remove what is not of you. I thank you, Lord, for the blessing of friendship. Amen.

Something to Ponder

WHAT THINGS DO GOOD FRIENDS DO TOGETHER?

Singleness

MARLOW SHIELDS-TALTON

Thou wilt shew me the path of life: in thy
presence is fulness of joy; at thy right hand
there are pleasures for evermore.

Psalm 16:11

Where to from here?

JIM JACKSON, CEO OF CHU FOODS, CALLED a board meeting with his staff one Monday morning. His objective was to find out where each of his staff members wanted to be in their career within five years. As the meeting began, he posed the question and gave directives for each person to write out his or her career goals. After the meeting Jim went to his office to review them. One in particular stood out from the others. It was from a relatively newly hired staff member, named Ann.

Ann stated that her goal was to be the next CEO of the company. She planned to obtain this not by fast-tracking but by cross-training in every area of the company. This path would lead to worth, and worth to promotion, and one promotion would lead to another until she reached the top. Jim was elated in that she not only made a decision for her future, but also devised a plan and how this plan would be executed. "These are the kind of people I like to promote," Jim said, as he smiled with glee.

Single people are looked upon as being independent. With virtually no one else to consider (unless you have children or a parent you are responsible for), you can chart your own course. With God's help, you are limitless. There is something

to say about being single as it relates to the question: "Where to from here?" Decide today that your "where to from here" will be limitless. Decide that the road to your divine destiny lies within your decision to be content in your current state of singleness. God sees, God knows, and God will provide. Decide that you will always go with God!

Prayer

Lord, I am your vessel who has the heart to live through every season that I remain single, whether it is by choice or because you have not yet allowed a mate to find me. Nevertheless, I will stand and endure because you have called me to great works even in my singleness. I will trust you to keep me and to lead me in the path of life and into fullness of joy. In Jesus' name. Amen.

Something to Ponder

WHAT ARE SOME OF THE GREAT THINGS ABOUT BEING SINGLE?

Meditation

MONIQUE HEADLEY

Give ear to my words, O Lord, consider my
meditation…Lead me, O Lord, in thy righteousness because of mine enemies; make thy
way straight before my face.

Psalm 5:1, 8

ℋ *quiet conversation with your soul*

I CAN'T HEAR MYSELF THINK...I SHOULD turn off that TV; it's been on for hours...I'll turn it off in a few more minutes when my show is done...I wish those kids would be quiet! I can hear them all the way up here from the yard...Oh, I must call the plumber about that toilet. If only my husband would fix it, we could save some money...I must remember to bring my checkbook to the next PTA meeting. I think I was supposed to pay for that field trip last time we met...hmmph, I wonder if Laronda will be there; she really made me feel stupid when she said...

On and on it goes, that internal dialogue that just won't quit. How can you get ahead when you can't even get the voices in your head to agree to talk about the same issue? Newsflash! It will never be easy, and there will never be breadcrumbs to guide you in the way you should go. But understanding an issue and seeking a resolution can be easier with meditation.

Meditation means being still, quieting down the chatter and distractions in your mind in order to just be quiet. It means focusing your heart and mind on God and resting in his love. Sure, sure, you can't be quiet when there are so many

people to see and countless things to do. But meditation is not a luxury. Meditative time is an essential tool to allow you to understand your place in this world.

Meditation allows you to mull over the events of the day, to come down from that jittery place, know that God is in control, and open yourself to the possibilities of it all. Meditation is the one thing you can do to understand your situation and seek your solution with the One who presents you with tests and paves the way for triumphs. Meditation is empowering. How wonderful it is to be able to gather strength and wisdom in the quiet moments of meditation.

Prayer

Lord, I humbly ask that you help me be as placid inside as the stormy waters you calmed with your words, "Peace be still." Please continue to guide me toward the path you intend for me. I ask that you fill me with your Spirit so that I may know your ways in everything I do. Amen.

Something to Ponder

HOW HAS MEDITATING ON GOD AND HIS WORD HELPED YOU GROW SPIRITUALLY?

Contentment

CHANDRA SPARKS TAYLOR

Not that I speak in respect of want: for I have learned, in whatsoever state I am, therewith to be content. I know both how to be abased, and I know how to abound: everywhere and in all things I am instructed both to be full and to be hungry, both to abound and to suffer need. I can do all things through Christ which strengtheneth me.

Philippians 4:11-13

Bloom where you're planted

SEVERAL YEARS AGO BRITTANY WAS required to move to a small town for her job. From the instant she set foot in the town she hated it. The people were slow, there was nothing to do, and the job was awful. She figured she would do her time there and get out. But God had a big lesson for her to learn.

For two years she stayed in the town because she had no other job offers. Instead of learning from her time there, she worried every single day about when she would leave. It was not until she learned how to be happy where she was that she was able to enjoy the wonderful opportunity God had given her. When Brittany finally understood that God was teaching her the secret of being content, she found herself enjoying small things about the town. She had a very nice apartment, the people at her job looked out for her, and she had developed several hobbies. She became so caught up in the joys of life in a small town that when she did finally received a job offer in a major city, she turned it down.

Many times we worry so much about what we don't have that we forget to take the time to appreciate what we do have. We receive so many blessings in our lives on a daily

basis, but many of us fail to recognize them. Even if you feel like you have hit rock bottom, remember there is always someone who is worse off. Even if you feel terribly discontent in your current situation, God has you there for a reason. Ask God to show you what he has for you. Then seek to be content right where you are.

Prayer

Lord, thank you for all of your many blessings and for showing me the secret of being content. Amen.

Something to Ponder

HOW CAN YOU RELEASE STRESS AND BE MORE CONTENT?

Community

VANESSA R. SALAMI

Thou shalt love the Lord thy God with all thy
heart, and with all thy soul, and with all thy
mind. This is the first and great commandment. And the second is like unto it, thou
shalt love thy neighbour as thyself.

Matthew 22:37-39

Valerie's little girl

SHARON JUMPED AT THE 11:00 P.M. KNOCK on her door. *Who in the world?* she thought, walking to the door. "Who is it?"

"My name is Valerie. I live right behind you. I'm looking for my daughter, Kiyana. Have you or your daughter seen her today?"

Sharon flung the door open at the sound of her neighbor's quivering voice. "No. No. I haven't seen... What's your daughter's name again?"

"Kiyana. I have told her a million times not to leave the house before I get home from work. There's nothing but trouble out here in the streets for a 12-year-old girl. I told her that. She just won't listen to me." Valerie's desperate eyes glassed over with tears.

"Here's my phone number. Please call me if you see my daughter. Please." Valerie left.

Sharon closed and leaned against the door. *It is truly a shame that I do not even know my own next-door neighbor or her kids. I blew the second greatest commandment to love my neighbor as myself.*

Jesus singles out the two greatest commandments ever given to mankind: 1) love God with all of your heart, soul, and mind, and 2) love your neighbor as yourself. Are you living

up to the second greatest commandment of your Lord and Savior?

Jesus' definition of a neighbor can be found in the parable of the good Samaritan (Luke 10:29ff). Every day of your life you are surrounded by neighbors—at the grocery story, at school, at work. Everyone you encounter is your neighbor.

Once you have committed yourself to making God (who is Love—1 John 4:8) the center of your life, then you should become compassionate and merciful to your neighbors. Try to develop the spirit of being the neighbor Jesus commanded. There's no better time than right now to begin doing what God commanded.

Prayer

Help me, dear God, to obey your commandment to love my neighbor as myself. Fill me with a loving and tender heart. Most powerful and all capable God, help me to increase my love of my spouse, my children, my parents, my family, my friends, my neighbors, my community, the poor, the rich, the lost, and the saved. Amen.

Something to Ponder

WHAT THINGS CAN YOU DO TO SHOW LOVE TO SOMEONE IN YOUR COMMUNITY?

Trust

CHARLENE PRICE-PATTERSON

Commit thy way unto the Lord; trust also in
him; and he shall bring it to pass.

Psalm 37:5

Trust during trials

JOHNETTA HAD PRAYED ABOUT THE SAME personal problems time and time again. Still, her trials and tribulations seemed to mount, and she often cried herself to sleep. She told her closest friends how frustrated she was because it seemed God didn't hear her petitions. One friend, Sandy, was also her Sunday school group leader.

One week Sandy ended the Sunday school lesson by playing a song entitled "I'll Trust You, Lord" by Donnie McClurkin. Johnetta was surprised because she had the same CD, but she had never listened to that particular cut. The song asked a riveting question: What happens to your faith when life is extremely hard? The song brought tears to many eyes in the class, including Johnetta's. She knew her feelings were inspired by the words to the song. She also knew that truly trusting God meant a lot more than simply listening to words in a song. Trusting God during trials in life meant work. Johnetta knew she had to truly believe in God and trust him rather than fear.

Scripture tells us that our ways are not God's ways; our thoughts are not his thoughts; our timing is not his. Some things just need time. Even when your life hits detours, God still loves you and is protecting and guiding you. Trials in

life can strengthen us if we allow them to. James 1:2 says, "Count it all joy when you fall into various trials" (NIV). It may be hard to take that view at first. But if you trust in God and allow the Holy Spirit to lead you, your trials will become your triumphs. God shields those who trust him.

Prayer

Lord, help me to rejoice in you, knowing you are using these trials to strengthen my faith. Help me remember that nothing is impossible with you. Lord, remove my fear of the unknown and help me trust you completely. I open my life to your power today. Work mightily in me! Amen.

Something to Ponder

WHEN LIFE GETS CRAZY, HOW CAN YOU TRULY TRUST GOD?

$\mathcal{S}ex$

CHANDRA DIXON

Let thy fountain be blessed: and rejoice
with the wife of thy youth. Let her be as
the loving hind and pleasant roe; let her
breasts satisfy thee at all times; and be
thou ravished always with her love.

Proverbs 5: 18,19

A romantic gift from God

MARY AND PAUL HAVE BEEN HAPPILY married for five years. In the beginning of their marriage, sex was a major contribution to this happiness. Now after five years, three cities called home, and three beautiful kids, Mary and Paul just can't seem to find time for each other, much less for sex. Whenever they do get an opportunity, it's over in a flash and Paul ends up being the only one satisfied. Mary misses being satisfied and she prays each night for God to grant her the courage to speak openly with Paul about her concerns. She now vaguely remembers those times when sex was great for her.

Mary decides to confide in her best friend, Carolyn, who has recently ended an extramarital affair that she claims brought her and her husband closer. Carolyn tells Mary that she should consider finding another man outside of her husband to please her. "Besides," says Carolyn, "this new man will look to you as forbidden fruit and will go out of his way to please you. Husbands just don't always embrace romance and foreplay." But Mary loves Paul, and the last thing she wants to do is cheat on him. As a Christian, adultery was not an option for her. She prays for guidance.

God grants her the courage to break the silence, and she speaks to Paul about her needs and desires. Paul was totally unaware of how Mary felt. They both agreed to make more time for each other and to openly communicate needs and desires in all aspects of life. That night they took the kids to Paul's parents, had a wonderfully romantic dinner, and made beautiful love all evening long. Afterward, they got on their knees, held hands, and gave all the praise and glory to God.

God gave sex as a gift to married people for mutual enjoyment. First Corinthians 7:3,4 says "Let the husband render unto the wife due benevolence: and likewise also the wife unto the husband....The husband hath not power of his own body, but the wife." As with any gift, sex was not just given to us for creation of life but to be enjoyed as well. If your sex life with your husband is not on fire, ask God to grant you a match, take the initiative to light it, set it on fire, and keep God in your life to keep the fire burning. You get out of a relationship only what you put into it.

Prayer

Lord, I come to you today on my knees with a bowed head and an open heart, asking that you continue to carry me through these troubled times. I understand that my sexual desires and activities must be placed under your control so that I may find what I so desperately need. Give me the strength to be open and honest with my husband about this topic. Allow us to openly express the enjoyment of the gift you have given us. Thank you, Lord, for all your continued blessings. In the name of Jesus, I pray. Amen

Something to Ponder

WHAT ABOUT SEX IS PLEASING TO GOD?

Dependence on God

ROSALIND POLLARD

I am the vine, ye are the branches: He that
abideth in me, and I in him, the same
bringeth forth much fruit: for without
me ye can do nothing.

John 15:5

$\mathcal{G}$et connected to the source

WHEN I TAKE TIME TO COMMUNE WITH
God, I often use my portable compact disc player to
play worship music. After a few hours, though, the
batteries will run dry and the CD player will shut
down. That's how batteries work—they lose power.
I've found the electrical adapter to be a better
option. The batteries can do the job, but only for a
limited time. The electrical outlet provides an unlim-
ited, continuous source of power. The music depends
on it.

We need a continual power source for our spiritual lives as well. Jesus is the vine and we are branches. Sweet is the sap that flows from the vine to the branches. The branch depends on its connection to the vine and the continuous flow of the sap which brings nourishment. So it is with our dependency on the true vine. The gardener is our Father, God. The vine is our Savior, Jesus. He is calling you to abide in him, stay in him, remain in him, depend on him. Independence is the enemy that will destroy your life in the vine. Your continuous connection to the vine is imperative for your spiritual life. You must "abide in the vine...for without [Jesus] you can do nothing." Dependence on Christ will provide life, strength, protection, and provision— everything you need—when you need it.

Prayer

Jesus, I need to capture this truth in the depths of my heart. Free me from my independence and impart unto my spirit the reality of my need for you in all things, at all times. In your name, I pray. Amen.

Something to Ponder

ARE YOU TOTALLY DEPENDING ON GOD? IF SO, HOW?

Children

SHAWN EVANS MITCHELL

Lo, children are an heritage of the Lord and

the fruit of the womb is his reward.

Psalm 127:3

God's great miracle

DEVETTA HAD DONE ENOUGH READING and research on childbirth to write her own dissertation on the topic! She and her husband Ray had tried for seven of their eight years of marriage to conceive. Finally, she and Ray knew all their prayer petitions had been answered. Now, in a matter of days, their bundle of joy would arrive. The nursery was set, the child preparation classes were a breeze, and, yes, Devetta was grateful for her sister-girls who had gathered at her home with more casserole dishes than she could count. These tasty frozen meals would certainly come in handy in the weeks ahead. Lord knows, she wouldn't be able to count on her dearly beloved to whip up healthy meals for her and her nursing baby!

Filled with nervous anticipation, Devetta dialed her dear friend Karen, a veteran mom and newfound spiritual adviser. "Hey girl. Come join me for a big tuna salad and V-8 juice—and I mean a big salad; I feel like I'm eating for four."

Karen thought about how it wasn't that long ago when she thought she would never hear her friend's joyful voice again. "God is certainly good all the time," Karen quips.

"And all the time, God is good," Devetta quickly shoots back.

Karen continued, "You know, birth is truly the

most miraculous display of God's omnipotence. How could anyone ever have any doubt as to his power, mercy, and goodness?"

"Yes, Jesus! You certainly don't have to tell me— God knows I know," Devetta shouts. "You know, lately I just can't get enough of the Bible and all its references to children. I get goose bumps when I read such powerful verses, knowing that children truly are God's little messengers, sent forth to preach of love and hope and peace. I have absorbed such words so fully, so unconditionally, that I am engulfed like a mighty river...Oh, oh, girl! My water just broke. Oh, sweet Jesus. My miracle is about to take place. Let me call Ray; we will definitely have to put that salad on hold."

The giddiness or abundant joy felt by an expectant mother while awaiting the birth of her child is something that cannot be articulated the same by any two mothers. Yet, a common sentiment reigns that claims God as its navigator. It's a voice of reassurance that she is about to deliver his blessing; a child born not only to her, but also to his kingdom of goodness. The Spirit overtakes her and God's presence guides her to this feeling of total euphoria, for the Word tells us, "Happy is the man [and woman!] who hath his quiver full of them" (Psalm 127:5).

Prayer

Lord, precious Savior, I humbly thank you for this blessing you have presented to me. For the rest of my days I will honor you by caring unconditionally for this gift: my child, my baby. Lord, in the name of your precious baby boy Jesus Christ, thank you for entrusting me to raise this child to know and follow your Word. My heart is filled with such joy, and I am so grateful and humbled to carry the name "Mother." Hear my prayer of thanks, dear Lord, in the name of your precious Son. Amen.

Something to Ponder

WHAT CAN YOU DO TO NOT BE OVERWHELMED, WHILE BEING THE BEST MOM, GRANDMOM, AUNT, OR GODMOM YOU CAN BE?

God's Yea & Amen

MARCIA BROWN WOODARD

For all the promises of God in him are yea,

and in him Amen, unto the glory of

God by us.

2 Corinthians 1:20

All promises, not just a few

LORINA WAS LEADING THE MONTHLY meeting of a ministry group in her church when Janis said, "I am tired of buying things that just don't work. I purchased some software that promised to keep my address and mailing labels up to date, but it really didn't do all that it had promised to do. It seems that a lot of the people I know are the same way—promise one thing and do something else. I guess I just have to learn to accept it because that's the way life is," Janis sighed.

Quickly Lorina responded, "I agree that many people don't keep their promises, but I don't agree that we have to accept it." Others in the group joined the conversation. "You can trust your family," someone said, but that was challenged by a member who had been betrayed by a family member. "You can trust a Christian," another asserted. Someone else whispered, "Not all the time." On and on they went trying to figure out whom you can really trust.

Finally a quiet voice said, "You *can* trust God and God's promises."

"God's promises?" Janis asked.

"Yes," the quiet voice said. "God always stands on the promises he has made."

We can trust what God says. His yes means yes and his no means no. God is the original promise keeper and he keeps all of his promises. He promises in his Word that we will not be forsaken or left alone. He promises that his Word is eternal and will not pass away. In a world where things change in an instant, the Word of God is the one thing on which we can stand that is changeless.

Prayer

God, help me to remember today that you are the original promise keeper and that all your promises are "Yes and Amen."

Something to Ponder

WHAT PROMISE OF GOD WILL YOU CLAIM THIS WEEK?

Divorce

BEVERLY MAHONE

Delight thyself also in the Lord; and he shall
give thee the desires of thine heart.

Psalm 37:4

Be careful what you pray for!

AS SHE DOWNED HER FOURTH GLASS OF wine, Georgette's mind began to wander. When she was a little girl she dreamed of being married and having a man she could love and take care of, and vice versa. She remembered being 25 and impatient to find Mr. Right. That's when she began praying daily that God would send her a mate because church and the bar scenes just weren't serving her needs.

Then Daniel suddenly appeared in her life, and Georgette believed her prayers had been answered. He said and did all of the right things. Well, she *had* seen some early warning signs. He started breaking dates because he had to "work" late, and he wanted to spend a lot of time with the "fellas" instead of spending nice, romantic evenings with her. But those things didn't matter back then. She honestly believed Daniel was her refuge from a lifetime of loneliness.

As she poured the rest of the wine from the bottle, she realized that what she had thought was love was nothing more than an obsession to be someone's wife. And what she didn't count on was a divorce, and *not* living happily ever after.

So many times we think we know what's best for us, and then go to God in prayer for affirmation. Then when things don't go as we have planned, we question, "Why did you let this happen, God?" When you pray, it's important to remember to put God's agenda first rather than your own desires. Delight in him first, and trust his timing.

The Bible doesn't look favorably upon divorce. As a matter of fact, the Word discourages it. Unfortunately, we live in a society that is more secular than spiritual, and the dissolution of a marriage is almost as easy as changing clothes.

If God blesses you with a mate in holy matrimony, it's not his will to see it fail. He wants you to succeed! He has as much a stake in your marriage as you do *(Mark 10:6-9)*. But you know what happens, ladies? Some of us tend to forget what we were really praying for. Once we've got him "hooked," we start believing it was our looks or personality or sexuality that won him over. What we neglect to do is keep on praying *(1 Thessalonians 5:17,18)*.

Prayer

Heavenly Father, thank you for being the light of my life and the joy of my salvation. Thank you for loving me like no other. My heart is heavy, Lord, but I know you are the strength of my life. Thank you for your grace and mercy that follows me even when I don't deserve it. In Jesus' name, I pray. Amen.

Something to Ponder

HOW CAN YOU HEAL AFTER DIVORCE?

Purity

NORMA DENISE MITCHEM

For the grace of God that bringeth salvation hath appeared to all men, teaching us that denying ungodliness and worldly lusts, we should live soberly, righteously, and godly, in this present world; looking for that blessed hope, and the glorious appearing of the great God and our Saviour Jesus Christ; who gave himself for us, that he might redeem us from all iniquity, and purify unto himself a peculiar people, zealous of good works.

Titus 2:11-14

Lord, give me a pure heart

SALLY TRIED TO FEEL SYMPATHY FOR HER girlfriend who was fired at work, but she knew one of them had to go. The company was downsizing and Sally needed her job. She was really happy to learn that she hadn't gotten the ax. However, as a Christian, she felt a little guilty that her thoughts weren't totally pure. She wasn't sure how to act, so she went to her pastor's wife for counsel. The pastor's wife told her that we are to live pure lives before others, loving and encouraging them. She needed to act more lovingly toward her friend who lost her job.

The Bible says that Christ came "that he might redeem us from all iniquity, and purify unto himself a peculiar people, zealous of good works." What we accomplish on our own is hardly noteworthy. We try our best, but the results aren't exactly amazing. But with Jesus' help, our life's work can truly be beautiful. We can only accomplish something great when we carefully listen to the voice of God whisper in our hearts. Then we can go forward according to his plan and purpose. God doesn't call the equipped, he equips the called.

Prayer

Lord, please give me a clean heart. Help me think like you and act like you would. As written in your Word, I ask that you "cleanse me with hyssop, and I will be clean; wash me, and I will be whiter than snow...Create in me a pure heart, O God, and renew a steadfast spirit within me (Psalm 51:7,10 NIV). In Jesus' name. Amen.

Something to Ponder

HOW CAN YOU BE MORE PURE IN YOUR DAILY LIFE?

Righteousness

SANDRA G. GURLEY

He shall pray unto God, and he will be favorable

unto him: and he shall see his face with joy: for

he will render unto man his righteousness.

Job 33:26

Worry like a thief

HOW MANY TIMES HAVE WE AWAKENED
with a million and one things on our minds? And
among those things, God usually takes a back seat. If
the truth be known, we are all guilty of this neglect
at one time or another. Let's talk woman to
woman…sometimes we get ourselves into situations
in which we cannot see the forest for all of the trees.
Something has happened during the day and we cannot resolve the problem in the time allotted.
Concerns set in and we worry about our families, our
husbands, our children, our jobs, and our money.
These are only a few of the many worries that we
focus on.

*Why do we anguish over things we have no control to
resolve? We work ourselves into a frenzy worrying and forget
about the most important thing: our prayer relationship
with God. When we forget to communicate all of our concerns and worries to the Master (1 Peter 5:7), we become
weak and ineffective. When we become weak, we cannot fight
effectively. Then we are guilty of letting the thief in—the
thief who comes to rob, steal, and destroy our joy. This can
only happen if we forget to pray, thus preventing us from
putting on the righteousness of God.*

Anguishing about things we have no control over robs us of our joy. If we are robbed of our joy we lose our strength. If we lose our strength, we can't be effective. The righteousness of God is our strength. Pray, so that God will render unto us his righteousness.

Prayer

Lord God, our eternal Father, we thank you for your righteousness and the strength that gives us. We thank you for letting us cast all of our cares upon you. Lord, let us never forget that we can do nothing without you, but in Christ we can do all things. Amen.

Something to Ponder

HOW CAN YOU EXPERIENCE MORE OF GOD'S RIGHTEOUSNESS AND JOY THIS WEEK?

Self-Control

ANITA A. DANIELS

What fruit had ye then in those things
whereof ye are now ashamed? for the
end of those things is death.

Romans 6:21

Rewind

LINDSAY LIVED IN AN ATTRACTIVE CONDO-
minium complex. Her career as a corporate commu-
nications specialist had begun to pay off, and then she
met the man of her dreams.

They'd been dating seriously for eight months,
and she was convinced he would be her future husband. He said all the right things. They did all the
right things—attending church and weekly Bible
study, praying and reading Scripture together. She
thought they were a match made in heaven.

Then he became distant. Lindsay could not figure out what was wrong. She honored his request for
"space" to ponder their future. What she thought
would be a few days turned into a month. Her happiness started ebbing away as each day came and
went. And then she was shocked beyond belief! As
she was sitting in her rocker at 12:30 A.M., unable to
sleep, she saw his car parked at a condominium
directly across from hers. She had to be dreaming!

Seething with anger, she grabbed her robe and
headed across the parking lot. She started banging on
the door. When the door opened, she stormed past
the neighbor and found her man sitting in the front
room. Before he could react, she drew back and hit
him in the nose with the base of her palm, giving him
a bloody nose. She shoved her neighbor aside and
marched back to her condominium.

Since God was gracious enough to send his Son to die for our sins, do we think it is acceptable for us to keep breaking the rules? When we yield to anger, violence, fear, deceit, or betrayal, then we are slaves to our own passions. Instead, we can choose to yield to the fruit of the Spirit: love, joy, peace, patience, kindness, goodness, gentleness, faithfulness, and, yes—self-control. It's hard to fathom sometimes, but self-control is a choice. Lindsay relinquished self-control and succumbed to the flesh when she lost control of her emotions and punched her former boyfriend in the face.

Paul instructs us to exercise self-control and show the same zeal for righteousness in our new life with Christ as the energy we showed when we yielded our bodies to impurity and sin. Then he asks the question for which today's devotional is targeted: "What benefit did you reap at that time from the things you are now ashamed of?...For the wages of sin is death, but the gift of God is eternal life in Christ Jesus our Lord" (Romans 6:21,23, NIV).

Prayer

Dear God, please forgive me for allowing my emotions to run amok. It is so easy to believe that how I respond is caused by the actions of other people. Lord, I know you and I are in control of me. No matter how poorly another person treats me, I always have the power to resist the tricks of the enemy and respond with self-control, because I can do all things through Christ who strengthens me. In his name. Amen.

Something to Ponder

HOW WILL YOU EXERCISE SELF-CONTROL THIS DAY?

Holiness

SHA' GIVENS

With my whole heart have I sought thee:
O let me not wander from thy commandments. Thy word have I hid in mine heart,
that I might not sin against thee.

Psalm 119:10,11

Your words are weapons

CAROL ATTENDED CHURCH EVERY SUNDAY, arrived at work on time every day, and lived a simple life. She casually read her Bible twice a week, gossiped about her coworkers only occasionally when a rumor had arisen, uttered a curse word only when a car cut her off on the road, and had sex only once every six months when her ex-boyfriend was in town. Her philosophy regarding her lifestyle was: "Nobody's perfect!"

Becoming complacent in our walk with God can be dangerous. When we believe that we have done just enough to please God, and that we're okay because we've never committed murder or some other so-called "big sin," we can easily find ourselves deceived. The Lord wants his children to be holy as he is holy. While it is true that we cannot be "perfect," we should strive to please God in all we say and do. When we casually regard certain sins as not a big deal, we grieve God's Spirit. It is the Lord's desire that we change our attitude toward unrighteousness and do everything with the help of the Holy Spirit to walk in upright and holy ways.

Our faith in the Lord Jesus Christ is not based upon what we do in church each Sunday. The real measure of holiness is based upon how we conduct ourselves the other six days out of the week when we are not in the sanctuary. The

Bible says in Jeremiah 17:9, "The heart is deceitful above all things, and desperately wicked: who can know it?" We cannot trust our hearts or ourselves to decide whether we are in a good place with God. We must search and study the Scriptures earnestly and allow God to purify us from every unclean thing in our lives.

Prayer

Lord, it is my desire to be more like you. Show me all of my ways that are not pleasing in your sight. Reveal to me what righteousness and holiness look like, so that I may glorify you in every aspect of my lifestyle. Lord, where I have stumbled—forgive me. I need a heart change, oh God. Allow your Spirit to convict me in the areas that need to be purified. In Jesus' name, I pray. Amen.

Something to Ponder

THINK ABOUT HOW MANY SCRIPTURES YOU KNOW, OR HOW OFTEN YOU ATTEND CHURCH. DO THESE THINGS PLEASE GOD? IN WHAT OTHER WAYS CAN YOU PLEASE GOD?

Covenant

NICOLE B. SMITH

If a man vow a vow unto the Lord, or swear
an oath to bind his soul with a bond; he
shall not break his word, he shall do
according to all that proceedeth
out of his mouth.

Numbers 30:2

First things first

I RECEIVED MY UNDERGRADUATE DEGREE in journalism from the University of Florida. The majority of my assignments were written reports or stories. I often waited until the last minute to complete many of my papers, so I resorted to several devices to fill space in my papers. One of these devices was to define a word or concept and discuss the definition in the paper. The longer the definition the better! Often I found that one word can have several meanings.

One word that has a clear and concise meaning is *covenant*. A covenant is an everlasting vow, an agreement to be kept. A contract has terms and can be voided. But a covenant does not change with circumstances, and the terms are set from the beginning.

*Marriage is just such a covenant. In the Christian commu-
nity, a marriage covenant is made before God. With the
divorce rate hovering around 60 percent for Christians and
non-Christians, it is safe to say that many people did not
consult the dictionary before getting married. Maybe some
of us looked at the wrong word. Marriage is a covenant with
the terms "'til death do us part." The words spoken at a marriage celebration are called vows. Let's see how the Bible
defines vows: "If a man vow a vow unto the Lord, or swear an
oath to bind his soul with a bond; he shall not break his
word" (Numbers 30:2). God is speaking pretty plainly in
that verse.*

Prayer

Heavenly Father, we thank you for giving us the opportunity to show love the way you love us— unconditionally. Help us to remember that our marriages are to be imitations of the relationship between Christ and the Church. In Jesus' name. Amen.

Something to Ponder

IF YOU'VE MADE A PROMISE TO GOD, WHY IS IT IMPORTANT TO KEEP IT?

Confidence

RAYKEL TOLSON

Being confident of this very thing, that he
which hath begun a good work in you will
perform it until the day of Jesus Christ.

Philippians 1:6

Confidence in your purpose

EVER SINCE DEACON SMITH COULD remember, there had never been a funeral at First Baptist Church that Mother Jackson had not attended. Not only did she faithfully attend funerals, but she seemed to enjoy herself. While others would cry, Mother Jackson would rock from side to side with a smile on her face.

One day Deacon Smith asked, "Mother Jackson, why do you enjoy funerals?"

Mother Jackson answered, "A funeral is a happy occasion. Why shouldn't I enjoy them, baby?"

"What do you mean 'happy occasion'? Families have lost loved ones," Deacon Smith said with a confused look on his face.

"When a child of God dies, they are not lost. We know exactly where they are. They have gone home to glory to be with my Lord. I'm sorry that their family members are sad, but I know that they are in a better place. And one day the family will be reunited. You church folk make me laugh," Mother Jackson smiled.

"Why is that Mother Jackson?" Deacon Smith asked.

"Ya'll wanna go to heaven, but don't no one wanna die."

On September 11, 2001, the United States suffered a horrific tragedy. Thousands died. The deaths of those Americans brought grief, anger, and fear. As Christians, what will get us through the grief, anger, and fear is confidence in our salvation. Didn't we accept Jesus as our Lord and Savior to receive everlasting life? In John 14:2, Jesus told his disciples that he was going to prepare a place in heaven.

We should not live recklessly nor fail to take precautions that could prolong our time on earth. God has work for us to do on earth. He wants us to spread the gospel of Jesus Christ throughout the world. Nevertheless, we must not live in fear of death. As children of the most high God, we have nothing to fear from the terrorists of this world. If death is all they've got, let them bring it on. "We are confident, I say, and willing rather to be absent from the body, and to be present with the Lord" (2 Corinthians 5:8).

Prayer

Lord, thank you for Jesus and for the promise of everlasting life. I thank you for preparing a home for me in heaven. I will not live in fear of death. I will live an abundant life while I am here on earth. I will share the love of Jesus with others. In the name of Jesus, I will be confident in my salvation. Amen.

Something to Ponder

WHAT KEEPS YOU FROM BEING CONFIDENT IN YOUR SALVATION IN CHRIST?

Husbands

JAMELL MEEKS

And he spake a parable unto them to this end,

that men ought always to pray, and not to faint.

Luke 18:1

Pray for your husband

MELISSA KNELT DOWN TO PRAY WITH HER
prayer partner, a godly older woman. She began,
"Lord, make my husband more sensible, and get him
for the rude remarks he made about me at dinner
yesterday. Lord, could you make him a better Sunday
school teacher so the class will be more exciting? My
husband really needs your blessings. In the name of
Jesus, I pray, Amen!"

As Melissa rose from her knees, her prayer partner said lovingly, "Now let's pray *for* your husband."

*Melissa, like so many other wives, had begun to pray on her
husband, "Lord, get him for all the things he does wrong,"
instead of praying for him. It is easy to fall into a practice
of rehearsing our partner's faults rather than praying for his
needs and his walk with God. Luke 18:1 says we ought
always to pray and not faint. What does it mean to faint? It
means to give in to the flesh, responding selfishly to situations. We must fight the urge to give in to our selfish desires
even when we pray!*

*Praying directly from the Word of God about our situ-
ations and our family will bless our husbands and us. "So
shall my word be that goeth forth out of my mouth: it shall
not return unto me void, but it shall accomplish that which*

I please, and it shall prosper in the thing whereto I sent it"
(Isaiah 55:11).

Prayer

Father God, in the matchless name of Jesus I come to you today, trusting and believing your Word. I pray that my husband shall know the truth and that the truth shall make him free (John 8:32). Lord, I pray that my husband will humble himself under the mighty hand of God, that you may exalt him in due time. May he cast all his cares upon you, for you care for him (1 Peter 5:6, 7). Amen.

Something to Ponder

WHAT CAN YOU DO TO BE A BETTER WIFE? IF YOU DON'T HAVE A HUSBAND, HOW CAN YOU PRAY FOR THOSE IN YOUR FAMILY?

Seeking God

MARY BOSTON

But seek ye first the kingdom of God, and
His righteousness; and all these things
shall be added unto you.

Matthew 6:33

Focus on God

MY DREAM AS A YOUNG GIRL PLAYING WITH coke-bottle, straw-haired dolls was to someday become a mother. As I grew beyond those early years, the hope of earnestly and sincerely giving of myself to nurture a tender seedling placed in my care by God occupied many of my thoughts.

Our first child, a son, came seemingly without much effort on our part; just sheer biology. However it was to be ten years later before God intervened and blessed us with our second child, a daughter. I always thought that as easy as it seemed to conceive our son, the same would happen when we decided to have our second child. Why did the ugly head of infertility rear itself to thwart our plans? We so desperately wanted to fill our home with children, but we had to admit that our plans and our timing are not always the plans, timing, and perfect will of our Lord.

There were many sad days when hope was waning and my dream of another child seemed impossible. I shared my sadness with my praying friends, but my desire for a little girl only grew stronger. One day, in the quietness of my home, the Spirit of the Lord whispered in my spirit, "Just leave this to me. Trust me." Month after month and year after year, the message came: "Seek first the kingdom." I came to realize that all of my dreams and desires were secondary to my relationship with Christ. I also came to understand that I had allowed other things to become the center of my life and to dominate my thoughts and actions. The Lord wants 100 percent of our lives. Once I began to really know the Savior, it no longer mattered what my dreams were—I wanted his will for my life. He knew the desire of my heart and once we were in right relationship, he honored that desire.

Whether you are going through a period of infertility or any other problem that dominates your thoughts and energy, redirect your focus toward the Lord and his Word first and foremost. God is a jealous God. He demands that we place him in the center of our marriages, our homes, and our relationships. We can know his will if we seek him first, study his Word, and build a relationship with him. Surround yourself with praying Christians who can hold you up in prayer if you lose your hope, or your faith does not appear strong. Stand on his Word. Don't give up your dreams but allow God to minister to you as you seek him and wait for his divine intervention in your life.

Prayer

Dear Lord, forgive me for placing the cares of this world before you. I do love you and want to please you. I worship and adore you. I pray for your will to be done in my life and I yield myself to you. I pray for other people who are carrying the burden of unfulfilled dreams and hopes. Draw them nearer to you and bless them. Amen.

Something to Ponder

IN WHAT WAYS WILL YOU SEEK GOD TODAY?

Women of God

COLLEEN BIRCHETT

The fear of the Lord is the beginning
of knowledge; but fools despise wisdom
and instruction.

Proverbs 1:7

Tell o' Pharaoh

THE BIBLE TELLS A STORY ABOUT AN
African princess who wasn't afraid to stand up and do
what was right. The time was when ancient Egypt
ruled over the Israelites, who had suffered as slaves
for hundreds of years. One day, "the daughter of
Pharaoh came down to wash herself at the river; and
her maidens walked along by the river's side; and
when she saw the ark among the flags, she sent her
maid to fetch it. And when she had opened it, she saw
the child: and, behold, the babe wept. And she had
compassion on him, and said, This is one of the
Hebrews' children…And the child grew, and she
brought him unto Pharaoh's daughter, and he became
her son. And she called his name Moses: and she said,
Because I drew him out of the water" (Exodus 2:5-
6,10). By her courageous act, God used this woman
to make a difference in freeing an enslaved people.

Audley Eloise Moore, born in 1898, grew up
hearing stories and seeing brutality against African-
Americans. Her grandfather had been lynched and the
women of his household had been raped. It wasn't
long before struggle against oppression had become
her life. She fought to change laws that would affect
African-American children. She fought for the edu-
cation of black students in Brooklyn and New York.
She organized demonstrations in favor of black rights
and helped establish a soup kitchen in Harlem for

African students. When she was seventy-four years old, the Ashanti tribe in Ghana honored Audley Moore by changing her name to "Queen Mother Moore." Before she died in 1997 she said, "I have done my best to measure up to qualify as a woman in the Black Movement. I have done my best."

In these stories we see two African women, separated by almost three thousand years, living within vastly different cultures. One was a woman from a privileged background; the other was from a background of poverty and abuse. Both were surrounded by danger. In both cases their very own lives could have been at risk. Yet we see these two powerful black women take a stand—a public stand. These two women are not unlike hundreds and thousands of African-American women who work in environments where they must struggle on behalf of the oppressed. Unlike in the days of Pharaoh's daughter or in Queen Mother Moore's early years, many of us are in positions of high esteem, inside and outside of various political parties. What does it take to stand up for righteousness, even when it means possibly losing our jobs? The first place to begin, it seems, is with the fear of the Lord. If one fears the Lord, more than one fears human beings, one can act out of an energy that comes from a power outside of oneself.

Prayer

Lord, I have heard it said so many times that to whom much is given, much is expected. I have so much for which to be thankful. I have so much that my foremothers and forefathers didn't have. Yet I am rich in the examples they left me. Sometimes it seems that the risks involved in standing up for the next generation are too high. Please give me, this day, the strength I need to do you proud, and to make all of the strong black women that have gone before me proud. Amen.

Something to Ponder

HOW CAN YOU BE MORE LIKE THE WOMEN OF GOD DISCUSSED HERE?

Purpose

MONTRIE RUCKER ADAMS

But as it is written, eye hath not seen, nor
ear heard, neither have entered into the
heart of man, the things which God hath
prepared for them that love him.

1 Corinthians 2:9

Conceiving the dream

SINCE SHE WAS NINE, LYDIA KNEW SHE wanted to be a doctor. She enjoyed visits with Dr. Baker, her pediatrician. Dr. Baker was a beautiful woman with a dark complexion just like hers. She had a soft and gentle nature and a sincere smile. Whatever Dr. Baker prescribed, worked. If she had a sore throat, a stomachache, or the flu, Dr. Baker had the cure.

On television Lydia passionately watched the medical shows. There were dramas about the emergency rooms, family practitioners, and emergency medical technicians. Documentaries showed details of the human body, the latest in pharmaceuticals, medical procedures, and technology. She was intrigued by the thought of saving a life. Lydia knew what she wanted—and she wanted it so bad, she could taste it.

God created everything and everyone with and for a purpose. He knew what your purpose on this earth would be before you were conceived. God says in his Word, "Before I formed thee in the belly I knew thee; and before thou camest forth out of the womb I sanctified thee" (Jeremiah 1:5). He said he will give you the desires of your heart: "Delight thyself also in the Lord: and he shall give thee the desires of

*thine heart" (Psalms 37:4). This means that the desire you
have to glorify God is a desire he put in you. He wants you
to fulfill your desires and purpose in him.*

*Just as a woman's desire to have a child leads to con-
ception, our strong desire to fulfill our purpose in life begins
when our minds conceive it. When a woman conceives, she is
full of anticipation and love. She dreams of how her life will
be more fulfilled with this new baby to love. The ultrasound
she sees, the movement she feels, and the heartbeat she hears
give her confidence that her child is healthy. So it is with
our dreams. The desire in our hearts, along with the promises of God, allow us to step out on faith.*

Prayer

Heavenly Father, thank you for creating me with a purpose and for the desire to fulfill that purpose. I look to you for complete help and understanding. I know the road will be difficult, but you are with me. You are an awesome God, worthy of all praise. Please lead me and guide me in the direction you want me to go. I give all glory to you. In Jesus' name. Amen.

Something to Ponder

WHAT CAN YOU DO TO DISCOVER GOD'S PURPOSE FOR YOU?

Adultery

JAQUELIN S. MCCORD

If any brother hath a wife that believeth not,
and she be pleased to dwell with him, let him
not put her away. And the woman which hath a
husband who believeth not, and if he be pleased
to dwell with her, let her not leave him. For the
unbelieving husband is sanctified by the wife, and
the unbelieving wife is sanctified by the husband…
But if the unbelieving depart, let him depart.

1 Corinthians 7:12-15

Opening the cage door

WINSTON AND OLIVIA HAD BEEN MARRIED for seven years. In the past year Winston had changed from a warm and loving husband to a cold and distant partner. Olivia prayed for Winston and their marriage every day. She did everything she knew to do to please him—cooking meals, keeping the house clean, "keeping herself." She also worked full-time. There was no change in his attitude toward her, and lately he was staying out later and later. Olivia often cried herself to sleep but continued to do what she could to keep her marriage intact.

One evening Winston announced that he was leaving. He had found another woman with whom he had been having an affair. He was tired of hiding and feeling guilty about it. She was the one he wanted now and he was going to move in with her. Olivia was stunned; this couldn't be happening. She loved Winston and she took her marriage vows seriously. She was in it for the long haul, " 'til death do us part."

She sat motionless, tears rolling down her cheeks. When she saw Winston leaving, she began to sob, begging him, "Please, please don't go."

"I'm sorry, Olivia. I don't want to cause you any more pain than I already have. I have to go now." He walked out, closing the door behind him.

In his book, Love Must Be Tough, *James Dobson says:*

> *Of all the forms of disdain that one individual can show for another, there is none more profound than blatant infidelity...What can be done?* The answer requires the vulnerable spouse to open the cage door and let the trapped partner out! *All the techniques of containment must end immediately, including manipulative grief, anger, guilt and appeasement. Begging, pleading, crying, hand-wringing and playing the role of the doormat are equally destructive. There may be a time and place for strong feelings to be expressed and there may be an occasion for quiet tolerance. But these responses must not be used as persuasive devices to hold the drifting partner against his or her will.*

The truth is that loving someone is not enough to make him love you back. You cannot use love, money, sex, acts of kindness, etc. to make him love you. If you do, you are subject to being used, taken advantage of, and still not getting what you want out of the relationship. It is what is in the person's heart that will determine how he feels about you.

You may be going through a difficult time in your life, in your marriage, or in other relationships. Know that God loves you, but even God will not force you to love him. He gives you the freedom to choose him of your own free will. You must allow those you love, the same choice to love you.

Prayer

Lord, you said, "My peace I leave with you," and you left the Holy Spirit to comfort us when we are hurting. We ask that you comfort us today and give us your peace. Thank you for your love. Thank you for giving us the choice to love you of our own free will. Help us to love those who have hurt us with the love of Jesus, and to give them the freedom to love us back. Amen.

Something to Ponder

THOUGH YOU MAY NOT BE COMPLETELY SATISFIED IN YOUR RELATIONSHIP, HOW CAN YOU REMAIN TRUE TO IT?

Kindness

PAMELA ROLLINS

But after that the kindness and love of God
our Savior toward man appeared, Not by
works of righteous which we have done but
according to his mercy he saved us...

Titus 3:4,5

The nature of God

NIKISHA VISITED MRS. LOLA TWICE A WEEK at Maranatha Residential Home. This visit, she walked into the area where the residents were playing cards, singing, and conversing. She noticed Mrs. Lola sitting all alone in her wheelchair. Mrs. Lola was seldom asked to join in anything because she had a temper no one could bare. That didn't stop Nikisha.

"Hi, Mrs. Lola," said Nikisha.

Mrs. Lola squirmed. "I wish you would go away," she said. "I don't know why you even bother coming here."

"I bother because I care about you, Mrs. Lola," Nikisha replied.

"I don't see why, everyone else says I'm a grouchy old woman."

"Well, Mrs. Lola, grouchy old women need kindness too. Besides, you're not that bad. I enjoy being around you. Over the months, I have learned so much by visiting you."

"Like what?" the older lady murmured.

"I've learned how to look beyond people's faults, actions, or even their behaviors. I've learned to be kind to others no matter what." Nikisha continued on, "You see, God shows us loving-kindness in the midst of all of our faults, and we are to follow his example. We must love when love isn't given. We must be kind when kindness isn't there. And I've learned to do that."

What is loving-kindness? It is an attribute of God's character that is shown in how he deals with his people. Loving-kindness may also be translated as "loyal love." God's anger is for a moment, but his loyal love is forever. God's loving-kindness is a part of his mercy, and his mercy accepts and blesses us when we deserve to be totally rejected.

God wants us to show the same attribute. He wants us to be kind to others as a part of our heavenly growth. That way we learn to fulfill our destiny. Only as we allow the Holy Spirit to control our lives can we experience this kindness working in us. Left to ourselves, we sometimes find it hard to be kind. But when we surrender to the Holy Spirit and trust the Lord to work through us, we then become what God wants us to be.

Prayer

Father God, help me to yield to the Spirit inside and to use every situation in my life as a way to grow. Teach me how to show loving-kindness to everyone I come in contact with. In Jesus' name. Amen.

Something to Ponder

WHAT ARE SOME KIND THINGS YOU CAN DO THIS WEEK?

Ministry

EVELYN CURTISS

Therefore seeing we have this ministry, as we
have received mercy, we faint not.

2 Corinthians 4:1

Who, me in ministry?

THE SMALL ROOM WAS FILLED WITH LADIES expressing what they wanted to get out of the new Bible study class. Several expressed a desire to learn more about the Bible. Betty said that she would like to be able to teach others like Sis Davis. Kathy stated that she could never stand before a group and talk. Some of the ladies said, "I don't know what I am supposed to do because I don't have a special ministry."

These ladies were wives, single parents, career workers, and grandmothers. Their statements reflected timidity, fear, unworthiness, lack of confidence, and lack of training. The teacher told the class that there are many Christian women everywhere with shortsighted views of themselves. They don't see their potential ministry, which causes them to say, *"Never* could I do or be like her." The teacher shared that God has not called them to be like the "other lady." He has called each woman and gifted her with a special gift (or gifts) for ministry. Each woman has been given her own ministry to share the simplicity of the truth of the gospel. Therefore each woman had a ministry.

Today much emphasis is put on the word ministry. *Some women feel excluded or think that ministry is not for them. Others feel "ministry" is only done from the pulpit or when wearing a robe and standing before a congregation. It is my desire that God will speak to women everywhere, in all walks of life and on every spiritual level of growth, that true ministry opportunities exist all around them.*

Ministry is a very broad term meaning "service for the Lord." It does not mean just the office, duties, or functions of a clergyman or clergywoman (as commonly used today). The person who ministers has a servant heart. She will see opportunities to be of service and seize them. Whatever her gift is, she should give herself to it wholeheartedly. We are members of one body and members of one another, with many gifts to edify the body (Romans 12:5). Stop, look, and begin to bloom where you are, so that whatever God has purposed for you to do, you will begin to do. In this way your life will bear much fruit and the Father will be glorified.

Prayer

Dear Father, open my mind and heart to new areas of ministry you have for me. Help me to understand your plan and purpose for the ministry you have purposed for my life. Help me to accept your plan that I may be faithful in service to you and never give up. In Jesus' name. Amen.

Something to Ponder

WHAT IS YOUR MINISTRY AND HOW IS IT GROWING?

Power Living

JENNIFER KEITT

And Elisha prayed, and said, Lord, I pray thee,
open his eyes, that he may see. And the Lord
opened the eyes of the young man; and he saw:
and behold the mountain was full of horses
and chariots of fire round about Elisha.

2 Kings 6:17

What do you see?

THE PHONE RANG AGAIN. SUSAN'S HEART pounded and her stomach welled up into knots... again. Checking caller ID, she wasn't surprised to see that it was the mortgage company calling...again. They were three months behind, and the letter they had received last week said that foreclosure procedures would begin if they didn't catch up within ten days. Her husband had lost his job recently and they couldn't make ends meet without his salary. *How are we going to see our way out of this hole, Lord?* she asked silently as tears streamed down her face.

As she wiped the tears from her face, she heard her husband's car pulling into the driveway. She went to the door to meet him.

"How did the job interview go?" she asked hesitantly.

"They said the same thing everyone says... they'll call," he snapped. "I'm sick of this! Where is God when you need him?"

She knew exactly how he felt; she just didn't have the heart to verbalize her anger and frustration. "Well," she offered, "we've tithed; we've continued going to church; God will make a way." The phone rang again. Her husband picked up the phone and then called for Susan.

"Hey, girl, it's me." It was her best friend, Angela. "I have great news," Angela continued, the excitement hard to miss in her voice. "They loved you. They want you. They're gonna pay you!"

"Slow down, girl," she said, trying to understand what Angela was saying. "Who loved what?"

"Girl, remember that party that you helped me and my sorority sisters throw for the fundraiser?"

"Yeah," she responded, pulling the event from way back in her memory.

Angela went on. "Well, there was this corporate bigwig at that event who wanted to know who pulled our party together. When he found out, he asked how to contact you. He wants to hire you to throw his company's upcoming employee party. He said he's willing to pay you five thousand dollars!"

"Stop messing with me," she said, stunned.

Angela was thrilled. "I'm not playing; this is for real. God is awesome!"

Honey, when your back is against the wall, you can guarantee the horses and chariots of fire are nearby waiting to come to your rescue! God is not idle. He is making crooked places straight (Isaiah 45:2). Women who are interested in power living understand, trust, rely on, and apply this rule in their lives: He is our shield and exceedingly great reward (Genesis 15:1)!

Prayer

Lord, open my eyes. Let me see your hosts, your chariots of fire, your horses, and your provision for me and my life. I believe that you love me enough to deliver me from all my enemies or keep me in the midst of trouble. Lord, please help me trust you. I want to see my enemies defeated in my life. Today and every day I will walk by faith and not by sight, in Jesus' name. Amen.

Something to Ponder

WHAT ARE SOME POSITIVE SAYINGS YOU CAN USE TO REMIND YOURSELF THAT GOD IS TRUSTWORTHY?

Hope

JEAN ALICIA ELSTER

The people that walked in darkness have
seen a great light: they that dwell in the land
of the shadow of death, upon them hath
the light shined.

Isaiah 9:2

Making a way out of no way

TONYA HUNG UP THE TELEPHONE. SHE WAS devastated by the news from her daughter's high school counselor. Since the death of her husband five years earlier, she had struggled to raise her two children—a son and a daughter—in a way that was pleasing to God. She worked a job that allowed her to be home when her children got home from school. She was active in her church and made sure her children took part in youth group activities. Now the counselor was telling her that her daughter had been truant and had been caught with a group of other kids smoking marijuana.

Tonya sank into a chair and sobbed into her hands. She had not felt that much sorrow since the death of her husband. Then, as she thought about that past time of tears, she remembered what had comforted her: the knowledge that her husband was resting in the bosom of the Lord. She remembered the joy that overcame her as she envisioned seeing her husband once more in the heavenly Jerusalem.

Tonya stopped crying. "I will not be defeated," she asserted to herself, "because my hope is in the Lord." She wiped her eyes. She knelt down right where she was and prayed to God for hope and strength. As she stood up, the heaviness was gone from her heart. Her spirit was lifted. She felt the light of God shining all around her. She picked up the telephone and called the school. By the power of God, she knew she had the strength to help her daughter in whatever way she could.

Too often we are willing to let the burdens of life overcome us. We wrestle with problems using our own strength. We let defeat rule our lives. We listen to those who have nothing good or positive to say to us. We watch the turmoil of the world and accept it as our own. But the story of Christmas reminds us that our God is a God of hope. He does not will that we sink into despair or wallow in darkness. His will is for his light to lead us every step of the way, and that we walk through the world letting his light shine all around us. Jesus said, "I am the light of the world: he that followeth me shall not walk in darkness, but shall have the light of life" (John 8:12). With the Spirit of Christ within us, his light leads us from despair to hope. And that hope is what Christmas is all about.

Prayer

Dear Jesus, you are the light of the world. Your light is upon us and within us. Your light casts out all darkness. Your light gives us the strength to hope when others see no hope. Your light lets us live when there is death all around us. Help us to use that light. And then please, dear God, let others see that our hope comes from your light that dwells within us. Amen.

Something to Ponder

WHAT WILL YOU DO TO SPREAD LOVE AND CHEER TO OTHERS?

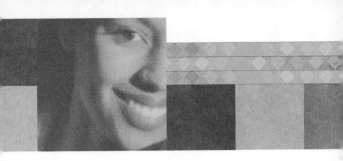

Self-Esteem

PATRICIA HALEY

I will praise thee; for I am fearfully and
wonderfully made: marvelous are thy works;
and that my soul knoweth right well.

Psalm 139:14

No accidents

HAVE YOU EVER STOOD IN FRONT OF THE mirror and wondered, Who in the world am I? How did I get here? Why am I here? Why in the world did God create me? Am I special to anybody?

Who hasn't asked those kinds of questions? It's a part of understanding our purpose in life, our place, and our worth. At some point in life we all yearn for a sense of belonging, a sense of worth. It's not uncommon for an adopted child to seek his or her natural parents, even after being raised in a loving environment. Why? Because we as humans want to belong. We want to know where we came from. We want to feel good about ourselves and to know that others feel the same about us. We want to know that we do matter, that our living is worthwhile and has direction. Before you can figure out where you're headed, it helps to know from where you've come. Knowing that there is an awesome God who created you in his image stimulates a proud feeling. The thought of how phenomenal you are, because of the blueprint that was used to create you, is overwhelming.

Nothing that you were born with was by accident. I have an unusual birthmark between my nose and lip. In the winter it gets darker, and it gets lighter in the summer. Most people mistake it for a lipstick mark. It's quite noticeable and always attracts attention. I'm not sure why God gave it to me, but since he did, I know that it was uniquely and wonderfully placed on my face and has a specific purpose.

So the next time you stand at the mirror and wonder who you are, joyously respond by saying, "I am the creation of a perfectly awesome God who made me in his image for a purpose, physical flaws and all. I do indeed matter, and I am worthwhile."

In order to have positive self-esteem, which equates to a positive self-image, you must understand who you are. Take a moment to meditate on the image of an awesome God making and shaping you to be just exactly as you are. Write down five characteristics, features, or emotions that God made unique to you. Then give some thought to realizing and fulfilling your purpose.

Prayer

Father, you made me in your image, perfect and wondrously made. Help me to know that deep down in my spirit and soul. I also know that you created me for a purpose. I ask that you reveal that purpose to me. Lord, help me to understand who I am. In Jesus' name. Amen.

Something to Ponder

WHAT ARE YOUR GREAT QUALITIES AND HOW CAN YOU USE YOUR GIFTS FOR THE KINGDOM OF GOD?

Joy

REGINA GAIL MALLOY

But the fruit of the Spirit is love, joy,

peace, longsuffering, gentleness, goodness,

faith, meekness, temperance: against

such there is no law.

Galatians 5:22,23

God's great joy

EVERY DAY AT AROUND 5:20 P.M. JOYCE picked up her three-year-old daughter, Jayla, from her baby-sitter's house. Right next door there was a sweet old man who sat on the porch in his wheel-chair. Each day when Joyce reached the front gate of the house, he would say, "Ain't our God a good God?" Each day Joyce would answer, "Yes, sir. He sure is."

One day Joyce asked her baby-sitter about the old man. Mr. Jim, as he was called, lost his wife to a terrible bout with cancer two years previously. Soon after that he was stricken with diabetes and lost his sight completely in his left eye and became 90 percent blind in his right eye. His health had deteriorated so badly after that that he was confined to his wheelchair. A nurse came by every day to help him with his daily needs.

"Wow," said Joyce. "You would never know that he's been through any of that as sweet as he is." Her baby-sitter agreed, "I said the same thing when he told me his story; and all he said to me was, 'Ain't our God a good God?'"

The Funk & Wagnalls Dictionary *defines the word* joy *as "more intense than happiness, deeper than gladness, yet nobler and more enduring than pleasure." It sounds like even the definition experts have a difficult time describing joy, because joy is not natural—joy is spiritual.*

The Bible tells us in Galatians 5:22 that joy is one of the attributes of the fruit of the Holy Spirit. So joy doesn't come from an external source. It is an internal *spiritual characteristic of and from the Holy Spirit. Joy is that godly characteristic that will enable you to walk through the valley of the shadow of death, but not feel like dying. Joy is not the absence of trouble, but it is the absence of depression in trouble. And you can't make joy happen to you by changing your hairstyle or wearing new clothes or buying a new pair of shoes. Those things may make you happy, but nothing can bring you joy except the Holy Spirit working joy into you. He has to work it in you, and that work takes time. Thank God for the joy of the Lord, which is truly our strength!*

Prayer

Dear heavenly Father, thank you for being the only One who can give us real joy. Today I ask that, through the Holy Spirit, you continue to work your divine nature into my innermost being. Lord, continue to impart your love, and then fill me with your unspeakable joy until it overflows into peace, patience, kindness, goodness, faithfulness, gentleness, and self-control. In Jesus' name, I pray. Amen.

Something to Ponder

HOW CAN YOU HAVE JOY WHILE IN THE VALLEY?

Thanksgiving

SHARON EWELL FOSTER

Take therefore no thought for the morrow:
for the morrow shall take thought for the
things of itself.

Matthew 6:34

Thank you for today, Lord

GENEVA WATCHED THE SERVING PLATES being passed from hand to hand. Steam curled from the mashed potatoes and from the dish of candied yams. The tart smell of cranberry sauce made her mouth water. There were bowls full of greens and macaroni and cheese, and a platter with more dressing and sliced turkey than the six of them gathered around the table could eat.

All of them were talking and smiling, but Geneva wasn't sure if she should join in the frivolity. There was plenty of food here today; but what about tomorrow? Her own cabinets at home were bare— she'd eaten her last pack of ramen noodles for breakfast. It wasn't easy starting out on her own; with rent and utilities, food just didn't seem to be in the budget. There was plenty today; but what about tomorrow? Geneva hesitantly dipped a large spoon into the greens that her grandmother passed to her and took a small portion.

Grandma leaned toward Geneva and whispered, "Now don't you skimp on fixing up a big plate. You know I already got a little something packed up and set to the side for you to take home." Her grandmother smiled. Geneva nodded and looked down to hide the tears in her eyes. "Thank you, Lord," she whispered, "for my daily bread."

Rarely is our focus on enjoying the present moment——there are usually worries that get in the way. Most of our worries are forward worries; we are worrying about what is to come. Will we get there on time? What will people think? How will it all turn out? We think that if we are not on guard making sure that things happen, those things won't get done. Maybe. Maybe not. Most of the disasters we anticipate never come to pass. Our futures are in God's hands and he promises to meet today's needs today. Stop worrying; he will still be God tomorrow. Tomorrow's too big for us to handle, but God is faithful to give us what we need to survive today.

It is more fruitful to live in and be thankful for the moment in which we exist. We should suck the sweet juice out of each moment, nibble on each event, and savor the taste as it rolls around on our tongues. Instead of worrying, we should thank God for each moment and not sacrifice today's joy fretting about tomorrow. Take a lesson from Geneva—don't worry; enjoy the pleasure and hope of this day! Just like Grandma, God's always got a little something stowed away!

Prayer

Lord, help us to keep our thoughts where they belong. Bring to our minds pleasant things that are happening in the right now. Teach us to have thankful minds, hearts, and spirits that are grounded in our trust that you already have tomorrow under control. Amen.

Something to Ponder

WHAT ARE YOU THANKFUL FOR?

Homemaker

KIM JOHNSON

Every wise woman buildeth her house, but
the foolish plucketh it down with her hands.

Proverbs 14:1

Finding support

ELIZABETH CALLED HER FRIEND DEIRDRE. "Girl! What's up? We haven't talked in about two years. Time has gotten away from us."

Deirdre responded, "I know, but we can put a change to that!" and they chuckled. Their long distance call lasted for over two hours. The majority of the conversation was about Elizabeth's decision to change careers.

Deirdre said, "Are you serious? You are doing what? A homemaker? What made you decide to be a homemaker?"

Elizabeth was excited to explain to Deirdre how she and her husband, Eric, had committed their decision to prayer. They realized some people would challenge their decision, but they were eager for their family to grow as the Lord chose to bless them with children.

Today the greater challenge seems to come from those who either disagree with or don't understand the exciting priv- ilege of being a homemaker. Making the decision to become a homemaker is as simple as deciding to become a doctor or lawyer. In making the career choice of being a homemaker, the Lord is faithful to meet our spiritual, physical, and

emotional needs as we face challenges, insults, and people who do not understand why we are doing this.

In all challenges we should turn to the Lord for instruction on how to handle the specific situation. We are encouraged to trust in the Lord with all our hearts, to not lean on our own understanding, and to acknowledge him (Proverbs 3:5,6). We are encouraged to commit our works to the Lord (Proverbs 16:3). Lastly, we are encouraged to delight ourselves in the Lord, commit our way to him, and trust him (Psalm 37:4-6).

Prayer

Thank you, Lord, for giving me understanding regarding the ideas of achievement and success. Help me to see a greater value in making decisions in light of your truth. May you be glorified in the things that I do and say in my home and family relationships. Help me to make the most of every opportunity you grant. Amen.

Something to Ponder

WHAT WORTH DO YOU SEE IN BEING A HOMEMAKER?

Delight in the Lord

LADENA RENWICK

Behold the Lord's hand is not shortened,

that it cannot save; neither his ear heavy,

that it cannot hear.

Isaiah 59:1

When you can see God's hand

CAROLYN HAD GOTTEN MARRIED AT A young age. She had given up her dream of becoming a nurse to become a housewife. She stood behind Clarence as he pursued his medical career. They later had two children, and she was a devoted wife and mother. She catered to Clarence even though he was verbally abusive. He was indeed a good provider, and she felt that made up for his being abusive. She thought many times about leaving, but she had never worked before and felt she could not make it alone.

Slowly Carolyn noticed Clarence's behavior changing. Her woman's intuition told her that Clarence was having an affair, and sure enough, he was. He told her that he wanted out of the marriage. Carolyn was devastated. Eighteen years of her life with this man and now he was leaving? She suggested that they go to counseling, but Clarence refused. The very next day he filed for divorce.

She immediately fell into a deep depression. She prayed to God. How could he let this happen? What about their family? Later, one of her best friends reminded her of the dream she had given up. Now was the time to go after it and become a nurse. Carolyn got a job at the local mall, went to school at night, started going back to church, and rededicated her life to God. Times were tough but she kept going. Carolyn is now the head nurse in an operating room.

She thought that she needed Clarence, but God showed her that what she really needed was him. Carolyn now witnesses to the truth that when we depend on God, he will never fail us.

The Bible tells us in Habakkuk to write the vision and make it plain. It also says that if we delight ourselves in the Lord, he will give us the desires of our heart. Never put your hope in the wrong thing. Do not be afraid to dream. Know that God can make the impossible possible. Always give to others, but never lose yourself in the process. God will lead you, and you will be a witness for him.

Prayer

Lord, I stretch my hand out to you in my times of disappointment. There is no other God but you. Help me develop courage so that I may be able to face the challenges of life. Show me that all my security lies in you and that I am a divine instrument to show your glory. Amen.

Something to Ponder

WHAT IMPOSSIBLE SITUATION IN YOUR LIFE CAN YOU TRUST GOD TO MAKE POSSIBLE?

More Than Conquerors

WINNIE SARAH CLARK JENKINS

The woman saith unto him, I know that
Messias cometh, which is called Christ: when
he is come, he will tell us all things. Jesus
saith unto her, I that speak unto thee am he.

John 4:25,26

We can know he is real

A WOMAN HAD GROWN UP BELIEVING THAT God was watching, but from a distance. She believed that when God was done creating, he just sat back and watched what he created. She could never understand that God could be a participant in a world full of sin and deprivation. She found no evidence that Jesus was anybody but a good person who had delusions of grandeur. After all, he thought he was God. *Gee,* she thought, *if he were alive today, they'd be locking him up for perpetrating a fraud, or he'd be in a straitjacket.*

The whole foundation of Christianity is that Jesus was the Messiah written about by the ancient prophets. If the Resurrection actually happened, then Jesus is who he said he is. Christ's crucifixion is a matter of history, as is his burial and empty tomb. Jesus was hung on a cross until he died. With the permission of Pilate, his body was given to Joseph of Arimathea to bury. With the help of Nicodemus, Joseph wrapped Jesus' body in seventy-five pounds of spices in strips of linen, in accordance with Jewish burial customs (John 19:38-40). His body was then placed in a new tomb cut out of rock. A large stone was rolled in front of the doorway of the tomb.

In order to ensure that the prophecy about Jesus rising again did not come true, the Pharisees had

Pilate give an order that the tomb be made secure. They even put a royal seal on the stone and posted guards so the disciples couldn't steal Jesus' body (Matthew 27:62-66). No matter what man does, God is able. Nothing and no one can prevent what God wills. The next morning, the heavy stone was rolled away and Jesus was gone! No one knew where Jesus was except his followers whom the angels had told, the ones to whom Jesus appeared, and those who believed that he was the Messiah.

There was no earthly explanation for Christ's disappearance. We, as Christians, choose not to be limited by anything that is earthbound. We are citizens of heaven living in a foreign land who know and experience God's power in our lives. Christianity is the only religion whose leader, the risen Christ, did everything he said he would do. He even conquered death. Now he has made us more than conquerors.

Prayer

Dear Lord, I want to know you better. I want to know who you truly are in my life. I surrender myself to die to this world and be resurrected with you. Thank you for dying on the cross to save me from my sin and for rising again from the dead to give me eternal life. Jesus, I acknowledge you not only as my Savior but also as Lord of my life now and forever more. Amen.

Something to Ponder

WHAT DIFFERENCE DOES JESUS' RESURRECTION MAKE IN YOUR CHRISTIAN WALK?

Dating

JACQUELIN THOMAS

The simple believeth every word: but the
prudent man looketh well to his going.

Proverbs 14:15

Keys to a successful courtship

WHEN CLAIRE MET TOM, SHE ALLOWED herself to get attached to him emotionally before seeing what he was really like as a person. When Tom's unpleasant habits and tendencies revealed themselves, she ignored them. She believed in saving for the future while Tom believed in living for each day. His idea of saving for the future meant buying his dream boat. What's more, Claire was a people person, and Tom was not. He was fine on a one-on-one basis but when others were around, he seemed uncomfortable and often ended up being sarcastic and sullen. Soon none of her friends and family wanted to be around him.

Claire was nearing 30, and all of her friends were married, engaged, or involved in a serious relationship. She didn't want to be left behind. She continued to date Tom, while hoping he would change. Despite their vast differences, the courtship led to a walk down the aisle. Less than a year later, their marriage was shattered in divorce.

Developing romantic feelings for someone whom you hardly know can invite disaster—no matter how appealing that person may seem at first. Bad relationships more often than not lead to bad marriages. That's why it is so important to

get to know a person's inner spirit. Getting to know another person's intentions of the heart takes effort and prayer.

Communication is a very important part of dating. Misunderstandings can be prevented by not evading or glossing over sensitive subjects out of fear of putting your date on the spot. When asking questions, carefully note your date's reactions. Such discussions can bring to the surface qualities of the heart that should be seen before considering marriage with this person.

If you find that you and your date are looking for different things from your relationship, do not ignore these clear signs of impending disaster. Do not expect your date to change his way of thinking. For example, if he is dead set against a commitment such as marriage and you're looking to find a husband, he is not likely to change his mind. Calling off the courtship may be in the best interests of both of you.

Prayer

Heavenly Father, give me the strength to see myself the way that you do and the wisdom to recognize the mate that you would have for me. I seek your guidance in this relationship. If this man is not the one for me, please grant me the courage to end the relationship with peace of mind. Amen.

Something to Ponder

WHETHER MARRIED OR SINGLE, DESCRIBE YOUR PERFECT DATE. HOW WILL YOU MIX GOD INTO IT?

$\mathscr{S}$uccess

PATRICIA HALEY

This book of the law shall not depart out
of thy mouth; but thou shalt meditate therein
day and night, that thou mayest observe to do
according to all that is written therein: for
then thou shalt make thy way prosperous,
and then thou shalt have good success.

Joshua 1:8

There is plenty to go around

KELLY WAS ON THE FAST TRACK AT WORK. Three promotions in two years had her perfectly positioned to become a partner with the consulting company for which she worked. Kelly's business world was survival of the fittest, and she honestly believed that the Lord wanted her to be successful at her career. At work, Kelly had found other Christians and they had started a book club that met once a month. On weekends, she volunteered as a Big Sister, and she was active in her church and was a faithful giver. By all accounts, Kelly's life was one of success.

One Sunday, Kelly's pastor spoke about seeking out your divine purpose in life. Kelly figured she knew hers, but decided to pray anyway. She asked God to open her heart so she would know how she could use her life to serve him.

When Kelly walked away from her lucrative career a year later to become a missionary at a small religious school in Haiti, she knew she had done the right thing. When she prayed for direction, God sent her a message loud and clear. Kelly needed to give in a way that went beyond that of the average person. After five years of missionary work, Kelly returned to life in the corporate arena, but this time she combined her consulting skills with her missionary experience and created a company that specialized in not-for-profit consulting. Quickly her business grew beyond her greatest expectations, and it was obvious to anyone who crossed her path that Kelly was walking in God's will. It was clear to her now that there was plenty of success to go around and fighting for a few treasured positions at her former company was not God's plan for her.

Kelly learned that success isn't calculated by how much money you earn or how many things you acquire. Success comes in following the lead of God and allowing the Holy Spirit to order your steps. It is impossible to measure success as a Christian in the same way that we would measure success on the job or in our personal struggles. God has made it easy for us to "succeed" as Christians. The Scripture for today encourages us to be like Joshua and meditate on God's Word day and night. Then we are asked to be active by doing what is written. And finally, we are promised that if we follow the steps outlined in the Scripture, we are guaranteed spiritual prosperity. At no time does the Bible say that life will be free of problems or temptations, but it does promise that by aligning your thoughts with God at all times, you will, by faith, be equipped to experience Christian success.

Prayer

Lord, I want to live for you and I want my life to be a reflection of your will for me. Please show me the purpose for my life. I am ready to accept your answer and act on it. Give me the courage to embrace your answer, and take away any fear or doubt that would keep me from successfully living for you. Amen.

Something to Ponder

WHAT ARE THE THINGS YOU PLAN TO ACHIEVE THIS YEAR? HOW WILL YOU ATTAIN THEM?

Salvation for the Asking

DOLORES L. LEE MCCABE

And [Hannah] was in bitterness of soul,
and prayed unto the Lord, and wept
sore…Then Eli answered and said, Go
in peace: and the God of Israel grant thee
thy petition that thou hast asked of him…
So the woman went her way, and did eat,
and her countenance was no more sad.

1 Samuel 1:10,17,18

Salvation is for all

DEPRESSION IS ONE OF THE MOST PAINFUL internal experiences known to humankind. A woman spent many weeks avoiding friends and family. She refused invitations, often preferring to sit alone at home in the dark. She stopped eating, did not sleep well, and was unable to concentrate. She had a lack of interest in reading, entertainment, and social activities. During periods of isolation she had self-deprecating thoughts and often felt like life was not worth living. One day she picked up the Bible and found hope in the story of Hannah, the mother of Samuel.

If you want to know what real depression is like, read 1 Samuel 1. Hannah, who was barren, became very distressed about her situation. The Bible says she wept bitterly, stopped eating, and was deeply grieved. In Old Testament times, conceiving and bearing a male child was synonymous with finding favor with God, equivalent to gaining salvation. Though Hannah felt defeated, deflated, and disheartened, she was also convinced, convicted, and committed to a holy God who could do anything but fail. Through her tears she cried out to the Lord—and got an answer.

You see, Hannah's problem was deeper than being childless and bigger than concerns over human life and the things of this world. Her problem centered around her relationship with almighty God. To demonstrate how much she loved God, Hannah promised that if God gave her a son, she would give him back to the Lord. The child was a physical representation that Hannah had found favor with God. So she was ultimately concerned about her relationship with God. Her sadness created a genuine, sincere, authentic prayer that needed a divine response. Only God could save her.

We, too, need God's salvation and grace each day. No matter what our circumstances, it is our relationship with our loving, heavenly Father who will get us through. We have to pray to make it through the tough times, but the prayers must be sincere, genuine prayers. These are the kind of prayers that God hears and answers. God is calling us to be authentic. Pretenders will not make it in the army of the Lord. Hannah knew she had to pray to make it, and her prayer was answered because she did not fake it. Salvation is ours for the asking, if we ask in faith.

Prayer

Oh Lord, have mercy upon me. When I am distressed, hear my prayers. Forgive my sin and seal me in your saving grace. Thank you for your offer of salvation. I will be forever grateful for the sacrifice your Son, Jesus Christ, made to save my soul. Amen.

Something to Ponder

EXPLAIN WHAT YOUR SALVATION MEANS TO YOU.

Health

DONNA GREEN-GOODMAN

If thou wilt diligently hearken to the voice of
the Lord thy God, and wilt do that which is
right in his sight, and wilt give ear to his commandments and keep all his statutes, I will
put none of these diseases upon thee which I
have brought upon the Egyptians: for I am the
Lord that healeth thee.

Exodus 15:26

None of these diseases

MARILYN HUNG UP THE PHONE AND SANK into the chair in disbelief. "This can't be happening," she said out loud. "Paula and I are the same age; we've been friends all of our lives. She is too young to have had a stroke. How could this have happened? What about her kids? They can't lose their mother. And her husband, Joe. He must be devastated!"

In anguish she cried out, "Dear God, why are my people suffering so much from conditions like strokes, diabetes, heart attacks, cancer? How could you let these things happen?"

Disease didn't just happen. It was brought about as a result of conditions that occurred when God's people disregarded the laws of health. Unfortunately, today we are experiencing an epidemic of deaths from chronic illnesses. When you look at disease closely, you can find a warning to get things together.

The Bible says, in Exodus 15:26, that if we, 1) diligently hearken to the voice of the Lord, 2) do that which is right in his sight, 3) give ear to his commandments, and 4) keep all of his statutes, he will put none of the diseases on us that he put on the Egyptians, for he is the Lord who heals us. Scientists have dug up and studied Egyptian remains buried in the pyramids. Autopsy results indicate that many of those people died of the same diseases afflicting people today—diabetes, heart disease, cancer, stroke, arthritis, obesity.

When we were created, God did not arbitrarily throw us together. Instead, he got down in the dust on his hands and knees, so to speak, and with precision carved out these bodies system by system—skeletal, circulatory, respiratory, reproductive, immune, nervous, digestive. On every nerve, muscle, and faculty, he inscribed his laws, which if followed, would bring health. Then he covered this wonderful creation with dust-colored skin and breathed into it the breath of life. Don't you know that your body is the temple of God (1 Corinthians 6:19)?

When God awakened Adam and Eve, he gave them the plan for healthy living. He told them what to eat—a plant-based diet. He explained that the best exercise would be walking through the garden to tend to it in the fresh air and sunlight. The weekly Sabbath rest would bring a special blessing to them. If they trusted his Word and obeyed him...and stayed away from that tree...they would have health and happiness. But they had another plan, and you know the rest of the story! Are you living a life that is outside of God's plan for healthy living?

Prayer

Creator of the universe, I am sorry for not honoring my body—your temple—as I should. I humbly acknowledge my transgressions and ask that you will create in me a clean heart (desire) and renew a right spirit within me. I ask that you will heal me of all my diseases. Teach me thy way, O Lord, and lead me in a plain path. Empower me by your Holy Spirit to be obedient. Keep me alive, and I will proclaim what you, O Lord, hath done. Amen.

Something to Ponder

HOW WOULD YOU DESCRIBE GOOD HEALTH? HOW WILL YOU ACHIEVE THAT?

Goodness

CATHERINE ROSS

Or despisest thou the riches of his
goodness and forbearance and longsuffering;
not knowing that the goodness of God
leadeth thee to repentance?

Romans 2:4

To whom do you listen?

ONCE UPON A TIME, A LONG TIME AGO, there was a very angry young woman who regularly rode into the king's court and tore up everything in sight. One day she was caught, and she was to be put to death, according to the law of the land. But the king said, "No, we shall let her determine her own fate. On one side we will put people to praise her and on the other people to discourage her. I will put a cup of water in her hand, if she walks between the two groups of people and does not waste a drop, she will live.

There were people on one side saying, "Come on you can make it. You can do this."

On the other side they were saying, "You can't make it. You will die."

Well, she made it. The king asked her which side she had listened to. She said, "Neither, I just concentrated on the cup."

The moral of this story is: You have to decide how you want to conduct your life, and that might mean encouraging yourself sometimes.

What does that story say to us? God, in his goodness, some-times lets us choose our own way, too. And sometimes that means we go the wrong way, and his goodness encourages us to repent and go his way.

We have a greater power to win people over when we are good to each other, rather than rendering evil for evil or cursing that which God has called blessed. Our goal is to present our bodies a living sacrifice, holy and acceptable unto God, which is our reasonable service, according to Romans 12:1,2. We are not to be conformed to this world, but be transformed by the renewing of our minds. It is a mind thing—as you think, so you are. If you think you can, you can.

Prayer

Heavenly Father, in Jesus' name, help me to be all I can be. May your fruit of goodness abound in me so others can see your glory in me and glorify you. Amen.

Something to Ponder

HOW CAN YOU REFLECT GOD'S GOODNESS TO OTHERS?

Topical Index

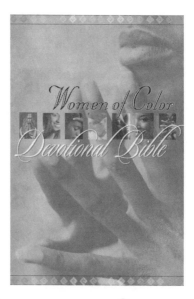

The first devotional Bible targeting African-American women

Fifty-two faithful women provide a full year of weekday devotions to help others deepen their walk with God. Each devotional includes an opening story, Scripture, application, and prayer, all revolving around a weekly theme. Topics, drawn from the Women of Color Devotional Book, include dependence on God, contentment, marriage, prayer, righteousness, and relationships.

ISBN 0-529-11583-2   Hardcover
ISBN 0-529-11584-0   Hardcover Indexed